To Larissa and Leo

Affectionately,

Maria Brendel

SYMBOLISM OF THE SPHERE

ÉTUDES PRÉLIMINAIRES
AUX RELIGIONS ORIENTALES
DANS L'EMPIRE ROMAIN

PUBLIÉES PAR

M. J. VERMASEREN

TOME SOIXANTE-SEPTIÈME

OTTO J. BRENDEL

SYMBOLISM OF THE SPHERE

LEIDEN
E. J. BRILL
1977

OTTO J. BRENDEL

SYMBOLISM OF THE SPHERE

A Contribution to the History of Earlier Greek Philosophy

WITH 30 PLATES

LEIDEN
E. J. BRILL
1977

Translated by Maria W. Brendel

ISBN 90 04 05266 6

To

Cornelia Brendel Foss

CONTENTS

Preface. IX

Bibliography XI

Abbreviations. XIV

  I. The Philosopher Mosaic in Naples I

  II. A Riddle of the Seven Sages 19

  III. Thales 41

  IV. World Spindle and Celestial Sphere. 50

  V. The Celestial Sphere of the Moirai 70

Index 86

List of Plates 89

Plates I-XXX

PREFACE

Otto J. Brendel died in 1973, two days before his 72nd birthday.[1] During his life in Germany, Denmark, Italy and the U.S.A. he wrote among many other things a number of substantial essays dealing with rites and symbols in ancient Greek and Roman art. These studies cover not only the whole era of classical art but include also manifestations of its survival during the Italian Renaissance. In his early thirties Brendel wrote an extensive study on the "Symbolism of the Sphere".[2] At a time when many scholars doubted whether archaeological monuments could support literary evidence, he used archaeological as well as literary sources in his attempt to give new, original explanations for a number of classical monuments.

The subject is of great importance for all students in art history as well as in classical religion and deserves to this day the attention of those interested in the cults of the oriental deities as for instance Dea Syria. Therefore it seems appropriate to republish Brendel's early contribution to classical scholarship which already foreshadowed his later work.

This new edition was made possible by the German Archaeological Institute in Rome which granted permission to publish a translation into English. Dr. Hellmut Sichtermann kindly supplied the greater part of the photographs. We owe the translation to Maria W. Brendel who thereby turned the "Kugel" into a "Sphere". The essay will now be more accessible to the English speaking world.

Mrs. Brendel wishes to express her cordial thanks to Andrée Conrad for her understanding help and suggestions. Special thanks are due to Mrs. M. E. C. Vermaseren-van Haaren and Margaretha B. de Boer who were most helpful in providing the bibliography.

Amsterdam 1977   MAARTEN J. VERMASEREN

---

[1] See now: *In Memoriam Otto J. Brendel. Essays in Archaeology and the Humanities* (ed. L. Bonfante and H. v. Heintze), Mainz 1976.

[2] See *Röm Mitt* 51, 1936, 1-95. For recent bibliography, see the forthcoming study of H. v. Heintze, *Zu den Bildnissen der Sieben Weisen* in *Festschrift für Frank Brommer*, Mainz 1977, 163-173.

BIBLIOGRAPHY

Bardenhewer, O., *Geschichte der altchristlichen Literatur*, I-V, Freiburg i. Br. 1902-1932, Darmstadt 1962.

Bendorff, O. hrsg., *Griechische und sizilische Vasenbilder*, Berlin 1883.

Berchem, M. van - E. Clouzot, *Mosaïques chrétiennes du 4me au 10me siècle*, Genève 1924.

Bernhart, J., *Die philosophische Mystik des Mittelalters von ihren antiken Ursprüngen bis zur Renaissance*, München 1922. (*Gesch. d. Phil. in Einzeldarst.* Abt. 3, Bd. 14).

Bernoulli, J. J., *Griechische Ikonographie mit Ausschluss Alexanders und der Diadochen*, München 1901.

Bie, O., *Die Musen in der Antiken Kunst*, Berlin 1887.

Birt, Th., *Alexander der Grosse und das Weltgriechentum bis zum Erscheinen Jesu*, Leipzig 1925[2].

Birt, Th., *Die Buchrollen in der Kunst*, (*Archäologisch-antiquarische Untersuchungen zum antiken Buchwesen*), Leipzig 1907.

Blümel, C., *Katalog der Sammlung antiker Skulpturen der Staatlichen Museen zu Berlin*, Berlin 1928-1940.

Blümner, *Technologie und Terminologie der Gewerbe und Künste bei Griechen und Römern*, I-IV, Leipzig-Berlin 1874-1887; Hildesheim 1969.

Böckh, A., *Die Staatshaushaltung der Athener*, I-III, Berlin 1817.

Böttiger, C. A., hrsg., *Amalthea oder Museum der Kunstmythologie und biblichen Altertumskunde*, I-III, Leipzig 1820-1825.

Cadion, R., *La jeunesse d'Origine*, Paris 1935.

Capelle, W., *Die Vorsokratiker, Die Fragmente und Quellenberichte*, Leipzig 1935.

Crome, J. F., *Das Bildnis Vergils* (R. Accademia Vergiliana di Scienze, Lettere ed Arti, Atti e memorie, Nuova serie, vol. 24), Mantua 1935.

Cumont, Fr., *Textes et monuments relatifs aux mystères de Mithra* I-II, Bruxelles 1896-1898.

Curtius, E. R., *Balzac*, Paris 1933 (trad. de l'allemand par H. Jourdan).

Deubner, L., *Attische Feste*, Berlin 1932; 1956[2].

Diels, H., *Doxographi Graeci*, Berlin 1879; 1958[3].

Diels, H., *Die Fragmente der Vorsokratiker*, I-II, Berlin 1922[4]; 1956-1960[10].

Dieterich, A., *Abraxas, Studien zur Religionsgeschichte des späteren Altertums*, Leipzig-Berlin 1891.

Dieterich, A., *Nekyia*, Leipzig-Berlin 1913[2].

Dieterich, A., *Mutter Erde*, Leipzig-Berlin 1925[3]; Darmstadt 1967.

Dörpfeld, W., *Troja und Ilion, Ergebnisse der Ausgrabungen in den vorhistorischen und historischen Schichten von Ilion 1870-1894*, I-II, Athen 1902.

Eisler, R., *Weltenmantel und Himmelszelt*, I-II, München 1910.

Elderkin, G. W., *Two Mosaics Representing the Seven Wise Men* in *AJA* 39 (1935) 92-111.

Frank, E., *Plato und die sogenannten Pythagoreer. Ein Kapitel aus der*

Geschichte des Griechischen Geistes, Halle (Saale) 1923[1]; Darmstadt 1962[2].

Friedländer, P., *Platon*, I-II, Berlin 1928-1930; 1954-1960[2].

Furtwängler, A., *Die Antiken Gemmen. Geschichte der Steinschneidekunst im Klassischen Altertum*, I-III, Leipzig-Berlin 1900.

Gerhard, G. A., *Phoinix von Kolophon, Texte und Untersuchungen*, Leipzig 1909.

Gilbert, O., *Griechische Götterlehre in ihren Grundzügen*, Leipzig 1898.

Goldbeck, E., *Der Mensch und sein Weltbild im Wandel von Altertum zur Neuzeit. Gesammelte-Kosmologische Abhandlungen*, Leipzig 1925.

Gundel, W., *Beiträge zur Entwicklungsgeschichte der Begriffe Ananke und Heimarmene*, Giessen 1914.

Helbig, W. - W. Amelung *Führer durch die öffentlichen Sammlungen Klassischer Altertümer in Rom*, I-II, Leipzig 1912-1913[3]; I-IV, 1963-1972.[4]

Huizinga, J., *Über die Verknüpfung des Poetischen mit dem Theologischen*, in *Mededelingen Kon. Ned. Akademie van Wetenschappen*, 74B (1932).

Imhoof-Blumer, F. W., *Kleinasiatische Münzen*, I-II, Wien 1901-1902.

Jaeger, W., *Aristoteles. Grundlegung einer Geschichte seiner Entwicklung*, Berlin 1923; 1955[2].

Jahn, O., *Die Entführung der Europa auf antiken Kunstwerken*, in *Denkschriften der Akademie Wien*, (phil.-hist. kl.) 19 (1870).

Stuart-Jones, H., *A Catalogue of the Ancient Sculpture preserved in the Municipae Collections of Rome*.
The Sculpture of the Museo Capitolino, Oxford 1912.
The Sculpture of the Palazzo dei Conservatori, Oxford 1926.

Kirchhoff, A., *Studien zur Geschichte des griechischen Alphabets*, Berlin 1877[3].

Leisegang, H., *Die Begriffe der Zeit und Ewigkeit im späteren Platonismus. Beiträge zur Geschichte der Philosophie des Mittelalters*, Münster 1913.

Liebeschütz, H., *Das allegorische Weltbild der hl. Hildegard von Bingen*, Darmstadt 1964 (Nachdruck der Ausg. Leipzig 1930) (Studien der Bibliothek Warburg. Bd. 16).

Lippold, G., *Die Skulpturen des Vaticanischen Museums*, III, 1, Berlin-Leipzig 1936; III, 2, Berlin 1956.

Lippold, G., *Griechische Porträtstatuen—Habilitationsschrift K. Ludwig Maximilians-Universität*, München 1912.

Loeb, J., *Festschrift für James Loeb*, München 1930.

Maass, E., *Orpheus. Untersuchungen zur griechischen römischen altchristlichen Jenseitsdichtung und Religion*, München 1895.

Movezs, F. C., *Die Phoenizier*, Bonn 1841-1856.

Otto, W. F., *Dionysos*, Frankfurt am Main 1933.

Panofsky, E.-Fr. Saxl, *Dürers "Melancolia". Eine Quellen- und Typengeschichtliche Untersuchung*, Leipzig 1923.

Pfeiffer, E., *Studien zum antiken Sternglauben (Stoicheia II)*, Leipzig-Berlin 1916.

Poulsen, F., *Delphische Studien* 1, Köbenhavn 1924 (Kgl. Danske Videnskabernes Selbskat Historisk-filologiske Meddelelser VIII, 5).

Preller, L.-C. Robert, *Griechische Mythologie*, I-II, Berlin-Zürich 1894[4]; 1964-1966[5].

Reinach, S., *Répertoire des vases peints grecs et étrusques*, I-II, Paris 1899-1900,

Reinhardt, K., *Platons Mythen*, Bonn 1927.

Reinhardt, K., *Parmenides und die Geschichte der Griechischen Philosophie*, Bonn 1916.

Reitzenstein, R., *Das iranische Erlösungsmysterium. Religionsgeschichtliche Untersuchungen*, Bonn 1921.

Reitzenstein, R., *Poimandres. Studien zur griechisch-ägyptischen und früh-christlichen Literatur*, Leipzig 1904; Darmstadt 1966[2].

Rougier, L., *L'origine astronomique de la croyance pythagoricienne*, Caïre 1933.

Salis, A. von, *Theseus und Ariadne, Festschrift der archäologischen Gesellschaft zu Berlin*, Berlin 1930.

Salis, A. von, *Der Altar von Pergamon. Ein Beitrag zur Erklärung des hellenistischen Barockstils in Kleinasien*, Berlin 1912.

Schlachter, A.-Fz. Gisinger, *Der Globus, seine Entstehung und Verwendung* (Stoicheia VIII), Leipzig-Berlin 1927.

Schneider, R., *Die Geburt der Athena*, in *Abhandlungen des Archäologisch-Epigraphischen Seminars der Universität Wien*, I, Wien 1880.

Schultz, W., *Rätsel aus dem hellenischen Kulturkreise*, Berlin 1909.

Speiser, A., *Die mathematische Denkweise*, Basel 1945[2] (*Wissenschaft u. Kultur*, Bd. 1).

Steinbach, E., *Der Faden der Schicksalsgottheiten* (diss. Leipzig), Mittweida 1938.

Stenzel, J., *Platon der Erzieher*, Leipzig 1928. (*Die grossen Erzieher*, Bd. 12); Hamburg 1961[2].

Thiersch, H., *Artemis Ephesia. Eine archäologische Untersuchung*. Teil I: *Katalog der Erhaltenen Denkmäler*, in *Abhandlungen der Akademie der Wissenschaften in Göttingen*, phil.-hist. Klasse, Dritte Folge, Bd. 12, Berlin 1935; Nendeln 1972[2].

Wiegand, Th., *Baalbeck, Ergebnisse der Ausgrabungen u. Untersuchungen in den Jahren 1898 bis 1905*, I-III, Berlin 1921-1925.

Wilamowitz-Moellendorff, U. von, *Der Glaube der Hellenen*, Basel-Stuttgart 1931; 1955[2]; 1959[3].

Wilamowitz-Moellendorff, U. von, *Homerische Untersuchungen*, Berlin 1884. (Philosophische Untersuchungen 17).

Wilamowitz-Moellendorff, U. von, *Die Textgeschichte der griechischen Lyriker*, in *Abhandlungen der Königlichen Gesellschaft der Wissenschaften zu Göttingen*. Philolog.-hist. Cl. N.F. Bd. IV. No. 3), Berlin 1900.

Wilamowitz-Moellendorff, U. von, *Isyllos von Epidauros* (Gedichte. Hrsg. von U. von Wilamowitz-Moellendorff), Berlin 1886. (Philologische Untersuchungen, H. 9).

Wilhelm, A., *Die Sprache der sieben Weisen*, in *Wiener Anzeiger* 16, 1922.

Willms, H., ΕΙΚΩΝ, Münster 1935.

Wissowa, G., *Religion und Kultus der Römer*, München 1912; 1971[2].

ABBREVIATIONS

AA	Archäologischer Anzeiger.
ABr	Arndt, P. - F. Bruckmann, *Griechische und römische Porträts*, München 1891-1942.
AD	Antike Denkmäler.
AJA	American Journal of Archaeology.
AM	Mitteilungen des Deutschen Archäologischen Instituts, Athenische Abteilung.
AmtlBer	Amtliche Berichte aus den Königlichen Kunstsammlungen.
ARW	Archiv für Religionswissenschaft.
AZ	Archäologische Zeitung.
BdA	Bollettino d'Arte.
BPI	Bullettino di Paletnologia Italiana.
BphW	Berliner philologische Wochenschrift.
BrBr	Brunn, H. - F. Bruckmann, *Denkmäler griechischer und römischer Skulptur*, München 1888-1947.
EA	Arndt, P. - W. Amelung, *Photographische Einzelaufnahmen antiker Skulpturen*, München 1893-1940.
GGA	Göttingische Gelehrte Anzeigen.
GGN	Göttinger Gelehrte Nachrichten.
JdI	Jahrbuch des Deutschen Archäologischen Instituts.
JHS	The Journal of Hellenic Studies.
JRSt	The Journal of Roman Studies.
MJb	Münchener Jahrbuch der bildenden Kunst.
ML	Roscher, W. H., *Ausführliches Lexikon der griechischen und römischen Mythologie* I-VI, Leipzig 1884-1937.
MonAnt	Monumenti Antichi pubblicati per Cura della Accademia Nazionale dei Lincei.
MonInst	Monumenti Inediti pubblicati dall'Instituto Archeologico.
NSc	Notizie degli Scavi di Antichità.
RA	Revue archéologique.
RE	Pauly, A. - G. Wissowa, *Realencyclopädie der classischen Altertumswissenschaft* Iff, Stuttgart 1893ff.
RepKw	Repertorium für Kunstwissenschaft.
RhMus	Rheinisches Museum für Philologie.
RömMitt	Mitteilungen des Deutschen Archäologischen Instituts, Römische Abteilung.
WV	Wissenschaftliche Veröffentlichungen der Deutschen Orient-Gesellschaft.

CHAPTER ONE

THE PHILOSOPHER MOSAIC IN NAPLES

Ever since the discovery in Torre Annunziata of a duplicate[1] of the Villa Albani mosaic showing a group of philosophers—incorrectly identified as physicians by Winckelmann[2]—it has been certain that both mosaics reflect a famous painting of antiquity. Furtwängler was able to relate the same picture to a representation on a Roman ring stone,[3] and these three monuments form the basis for any further research about it. Why did the ancients value this picture so highly? As an artistic design, the gathering of bearded men is not particularly appealing. The real interest of the composition must have stemmed from associations that do not reveal themselves at first sight, and which can be explained only by identifying the particular individuals represented and the special purpose of their gathering. As will be shown below, the mere description of the picture demands the recognition of a specific scene. The picture might well be the illustration of a mythical or historical moment or of a well-known anecdote, but it would still have to relate to some special area of ancient events and conceptions containing the hidden reference. At any rate, the original work belongs to that large class of paintings that have become indecipherable without their reliable titles. A riddle lies hidden in what we see, and this must be solved if the original spiritual reality of the work of art is to be at all regained from the preserved evidence. The present investigation is an attempt at such a solution.

The mosaic from Torre Annunziata, now in the Naples museum (Pl. 1), has been described by A. Sogliano,[4] but the pertinent facts may here be repeated in the interest of a better overview.

---

[1] *Mon. inediti* 1, pl. 185; 2, 242.
[2] First noticed by Sogliano, *NSc* (1897) 337 ff.
[3] *Gemmen* 3, 166 and 1, pl. 35, 35. Later literature on the Philosophers' mosaic: see notes 7-9.
[4] *Loc. cit.*

Overall dimensions: 85×86 cm ($33 \times 33\frac{1}{2}''$); picture without frame and garland: 64×65 cm ($25 \times 25\frac{1}{2}''$). Mosaic mounted on travertine plate. Tesserae mostly of marble, but with some small pieces of colored glass. Damaged mainly in the foreground between the scroll box and the sphere, particularly in a continuous strip of ground between the left leg of the leftmost seated figure and the feet of the seated figure on the far right. Restorations are negligible.

The ground is represented as a series of horizontal bands, rising from bottom to top in a gradation of brown to whitish tones.

In the left background is a structure of two pillars supporting an architrave on which four thick-bodied vessels are placed. Three of them have lids with twisted knobs. Next to it stands a broad-leafed black and green tree, its one barren limb extending left to reappear between the pillars. On the other side the tree's foliage is overlapped by a column rising from behind the figures, its capital surmounted by a sundial in the shape of a hemi-spherical bowl. A hilly landscape, apparently surrounded by fortified walls, emerges from the upper right corner of the picture. The small scale of the buildings and the blue tones employed between brownish lines indicate that the landscape lies in the far distance.[5]

In the middle ground is a wide semicircular bench, opening to-ward the viewer, with a low, rounded backrest running all around it and a pair of lion's-paw feet visible near the outermost figures.

The first figure on the left is a standing man wearing a yellow himation, its tip hanging down from his left shoulder. He has a short beard and wears a white headband, from which his hair protrudes over the forehead (Pl. IV, 1). The right hand is empty, perhaps in a gesture of speaking. He looks down to the man sitting next to him and rests his left hand on his shoulder.

The second figure talks to the first one, looking up to him (Pls. II and IV, 1); the seated man wears a dark yellow himation around the lower half of his body, leaving the upper half naked. His beard is gray, as is the fringe of hair around his bald forehead. He holds a scroll upright between both hands. His sandals are red.

The third figure (Pls. II and V, 1), a strong old man with thick

---

[5] Sogliano later corrected his erroneous description of the blue colour as water, *MonAnt* 8 (1898) 401.

gray hair and beard, sits on the bench almost completely wrapped in a dark blue himation, from which only his right shoulder and arm remain free. His left elbow is propped on the edge of the exedra. His right hand points with a long stick towards the sphere in the foreground. His head is lowered so that his eyes seem to follow this gesture.

The fourth figure (Pl. IV, 2), partly overlapped by the third and fifth figures, stands behind the bench—as is clearly indicated by the edge of the backrest. He is a bearded man entirely wrapped in a greenish himation, which he seems to pull together over his chest with both hands. He turns forward to the fifth figure.

The fifth figure (Pl. V, 2) is a man with a short beard wearing a dark blue chiton, over which a lighter himation has been thrown. He sits cross-legged and rests his right elbow in his left hand. The right hand touches his beard. The figure seems to sit not on the bench but on a slightly higher seat—probably the elevated pedestal in the center of the exedra, on which the column with sundial stands behind him.[6]

The sixth figure (Pls. III and VI, 1) is an older, bearded man, sitting on the bench. Barechested, he wears a dark blue himation around the lower part of his body. He props his bearded chin on a scroll held in his right hand. The left arm disappears behind the seventh figure.

The seventh figure (Pls. III and VI, 2), outermost on the right, is an old man standing with right leg forward looking toward the centre of the composition. The white himation, leaving his right shoulder free, falls over his left forearm. His left hand holds a scroll, which he seems to touch with one finger of his right hand.

In the centre of the foreground is a small box, supported by four feet, from which three quarters of a light blue sphere emerge. It is covered by a net of crossed red stripes.

On the ground in front of the man standing on the outer left side is a small box, with partially open hinged lid.

The Villa Albani mosaic (Pl. VII) must be studied under less favorable conditions than its counterpart in Naples. Composed of

---

[6] Petersen, *RömMitt* 12, (1897), 329. Sogliano, *MonAnt loc. cit.* 407.

slightly larger tesserae, the Albani mosaic was nonetheless carefully executed—again presumably on a stone foundation plate, although this cannot be verified due to the mosaic's present installation in the front of a cubic pedestal. The numerous restorations are extremely difficult to identify precisely, because they were done partly with the original stones and because the entire surface was subsequently repolished. We shall nevertheless attempt a description, based on an examination of the original by H. Fuhrmann and the author, in which those places will be indicated where the stones are more crudely arranged or unusually coarse, or where incorrect colors and mistakes in drawing occur. The following, then, is the result of our common observations.

Overall size: 66.7 × 67 cm (26 × 26¼"); picture without frame: 47.5 × 47.9 cm (18½ × 18¾"). Tesserae throughout are of stone, medium size. The use of glass cannot be securely affirmed.

The frame is mainly original and belongs with the whole. The black line around the edge contains several larger modern pieces, on which the small squares of the tesserae have subsequently been engraved. Bordered inside and out by a white strip and thinner black line is a continuous garland of grape leaves on a gray-to-black ground. The leaves are white, gray, olive green and ochre, with occasional dark green contours.

The picture proper employs a light gray background that becomes lighter toward the top without division into distinct zones.

In the left background are two pillars with an architrave supporting four golden vessels—all ancient except perhaps for sporadic replacements in the shadow of the architrave. There is no trace of the tree that comes next in the Naples version; this was apparently never included, so that the centre of the background is empty. Just right of centre is the column with sundial, less finely drawn than on the Naples piece, but probably ancient. A fortified wall with towers—but no hill—occupies the upper right corner. Below this is an architectural complex in which two rows of summarily drawn buildings extend down and forward from a structure vaguely resembling an amphitheatre. In terms of placement and color (light gray ground, white highlights, and dark gray shadows), these passages are of a piece with the rest of the background. On the other hand, the dark gables and two black lines on the long building to the right of the "amphitheatre" are certainly restored. A more precise statement about restorations in this area is not possible.

In the middle ground is a semicircular bench, whose roughly drawn lion's-paw feet are visible in profile on the left and frontally in the centre. A low, semicircular step serving as a footstool runs along the front of the bench.

The first figure on the left is a standing man whose white himation, bulging under the right breast, passes over his left shoulder to hang straight down in front. Obvious restorations: upper part of the head, nose, mouth, chin, and the neck down to the throat. Probably ancient, however, are the area of the face around the eye, part of the yellow-red headband, and the gray locks over the temple (thus indicating that the brown color given the hair on the upper part of the head is an error of restoration). The right arm is modern from the middle of the upper arm down to and including the hand grasping a snake. Here some spots have been painted over in order to conceal the rather coarse restoration. The snake was added perhaps because a fold in the himation suggested a similar line. The faulty folds in the back of the himation also suggest modern interference. The garment was probably longer. The feet and the dark ground line underneath them are modern. The left hand disappears behind the back of the next figure.

The second figure is a gray-haired man in a white himation sitting on the outer left side of the bench. Restorations include the lower contour of the face, the collarlike neck, and the entire upper half of the body, including the right arm. The lower part of the body and the foot of the bench are probably ancient.

The third figure, seated left of centre, wears a yellow-green himation. The figure is mainly ancient, including the sandaled feet and the section of step between them. As is apparently true for all the ancient heads, the hair and beard are gray, with dark lines indicating curls.

The fourth figure stands behind the bench. The section of the bench and its frontal leg are ancient, as are the upper part of the head and probably the right hand. The lower part of the face from nose to neck is modern, except perhaps part of the neckline. The figure wears a short-sleeved chiton, striped gray, red and yellow, and a yellow-gray himation. The chiton cannot be ancient, and the fold lines of the himation are disturbed in several places, but the precise extent of the restorations cannot be established with certainty. The right forearm is a modern restoration, but apparently a correct one, in so far as the figure rests his hand on the shoulder of the neighboring figure (No. 3) toward whom he leans and speaks.

The fifth figure, wearing an olive-green himation, sits beneath the sundial. The upper part of the head is ancient. Restorations include the lower face and neck, the right arm and shoulder, and the short-sleeved green chiton with red stripe. The left shoulder and arm are probably ancient, as are the lower part of the body and both feet. Fold lines are sometimes interrupted or shifted, and some of the contours have been strongly accentuated.

The sixth figure, holding a scroll in his right hand, sits with head inclined forward, looking toward the centre of the picture. The entire figure is probably ancient, although the reinforced contour of the right arm may be restored.

The seventh and last figure, wearing a gray chiton and reddish-brown cloak, stands on the outer right side. Only the stick and parts of the right arm appear to be ancient. The head is entirely modern, perhaps incorporating remnants of the original gray beard. Original fragments may also have been reused for the body, but the restoration is so arbitrary that the exact forms of the original figure cannot be determined.

In the central foreground is a cubic pedestal, resting on the ground on four simple feet. The whitish box casts shadows ranging in color from yellow to dark green. On top of the pedestal is a golden sphere.

For the time being there is little point in taking up the older discussions in which these pictures have been explained as Homer and Hesiod, the tomb of Isocrates, the Platonic Academy with the Acropolis in the background, or a fantastic School of Athens![7]

---

[7] Compilation Helbig-Amelung[3] 2, 460 ff. See also Schlachter, *Globus* 59. I am indebted to P. Arndt for calling my attention to Th. Birt's earlier interpretation and his later arbitrary identification of the standing figure on the right in the Naples mosaic as Aristotle, *Alexander d. Grosse* 471, 45. This

Although useful for the compilation of important material, these hypotheses have proved unworkable in most cases, primarily because neither the portraits nor the locality in question could be recognized in the mosaics beyond any doubt.[8] Furtwängler's casual suggestion that the seven scholars be seen as the Seven Sages has proved to be the most valid, and it remains the only interpretation that still deserves serious consideration.[9] In an ingenious extension of Furtwängler's theory, G. W. Elderkin has suggested that Demetrius of Phaleron, the Diadochus and learned collector of the aphorisms of the Seven Sages, may here be represented as a member of their circle or as the princely member presiding over a group of seven philosophers formed on their model.[10] By this theory, even the presence of the Acropolis hill in the background receives fresh credence. Although at first glance substantiated by the diadem of the leftmost figure, such an interpretation immediately leads to certain insurmountable difficulties. One of the few places on the Albani mosaic where the form and placement of the stones clearly indicate later interference is precisely the lower arm of the man with the diadem, including the hand holding the so-called snake. This same hand was the cause of Winckelmann's error,[11] and an authentic allusion to Demetrius' death by snake-bite[12] is entirely unlikely—to say nothing of the questionable artistic logic of making such an allusion by means of the instrument of death held in the subject's hand, for which no ancient precedent exists. The snake can now safely be described as modern,[13] as can the face of the same ✗

---

suggestion was also disproved by the well-known portrait of Aristotle. I thank L. Curtius for the reference to M. van Berchem, *Mosaiques chrétiennes*, XLIV and fig. II, and G. Rodenwaldt for the review by Wilamowitz, *Literar. Centralblatt* (1899), 91 f.

[8] Review in J. J. Bernouilli, *Griechische Ikonographie* 2, 34 ff.; Helbig-Amelung, *op. cit.* 463 ff.

[9] *Gemmen* 3, 166; *BphW* 20 (1900), 274. G. Lippold, *Gr. Porträtstatuen* 73 f. Interpretation as Seven Sages supported by reference to a mosaic in Trier, *Trierer Jahresberichte* (1908), 16. *RE* 2 A, 2253 f. Cf. Sogliano, *MonAnt. op. cit.* 392.

[10] *AJA* 39 (1935), 92 f.

[11] See above, p. 1.

[12] Elderkin, *op. cit.* 96.

[13] As already in Helbig-Amelung, *op. cit.* 462.

figure. As an Apollonian ruler,[14] Demetrius was certainly beardless
in the custom of his day; thus, if a bearded philosopher appears in
his place in the Naples mosaic, it cannot be Demetrius. In its
present state the Albani piece shows not only the beardless figure
figure with diadem but also three other clean-shaven men. By contrast the Torre Annunziata mosaic shows a gathering composed
of men with beards—throughout antiquity the most conspic-
ious characteristic of scholars and philosophers. We may therefore conclude that the four clean-shaven men in the Albani mosaic
are strangers in their circle; they do not belong here.[15] The blank
and inauthentic character of their facial expressions becomes
readily apparent by comparison with one of the better preserved
faces of the Albani counterpart, as on the seated figure holding a
scroll on the right. Furthermore, this figure cannot be Menander,[16]
since he clearly wears a beard in the reliable version in Naples.
Although little is known about the portrait of the poet,[17] it is certain
that he did not wear a beard and any image departing from this
convention would have been entirely incomprehensible to the ancient
viewer. The identification of another figure in the mosaic as Theophrastus can be refuted at once by a glance at the well-known portraits of this philosopher.[18] Thus these new efforts are futile, too;
once put to the test, the names of Demetrius, Menander and Theo-
rastus cannot find a place here. We must return, then, to the
starting point of this inconclusive excursus and to the only remain-
ing alternative: that the group of seven must be related to the
Seven Sages. We should by no means forget, however, that this
hypothesis too depends on evidence, and that a new question arises

---

[14] Elderkin, *op. cit.* 97.

[15] See above for description of preservation.

[16] Elderkin, *op. cit.* 98 f.; but the gesture of holding the chin with one hand
was hardly restricted to comic poets.

[17] See Crome, *Das Bildnis Vergils*, 28 ff. Even those who disagree with me
on Studniczka's dating of the portrait to the Augustan period will admit the
uncertainty of the earlier identification; cf. *Gnomon* 10 (1934) 233. The picture in the House of Menander speaks against it, but does not support Elderkin
either. F. Poulsen, *Gnomon* 12 (1936) 936; J. Sieveking, *BphW* 56 (1936),
338 ff.

[18] Elderkin, *op. cit.* 97. Cf. Helbig-Amelung, *op. cit.* 463. Portrait of
Theophrastus: *BrBr* 231/32.

immediately. The answer to it emerges as the strangest yet most essential problem of the entire picture: Why are the Seven Sages— if that is who they are—assembled around a sphere?

Since the sphere in the foreground is virtually the central point of the composition, it is logical to bring it into the focus of an exploratory investigation. First, however, we must attempt a more complete explanation of the picture's compositional relationships. What is happening? Turning to the mosaic in Naples, better preserved and probably more reliable, we notice that the seven men are assembled in a landscape. In the distance on the right is the much discussed fortified hill. It has no distinguishing features of the Athenian or any other acropolis. On the left, the setting consists of a sacred gate viewed obliquely, a tree, and a sundial on a high column. They too are typical but unspecific indications of locale, which serve to describe a sacred grove, an open-air sanctuary, or a garden.[19] The branch of the tree seen through the gate is a frequent motif of Roman-Hellenistic architectural painting,[20] and the golden or bronze vessels on the architrave are offerings of a type well known since Hellenistic times.[21] Also at home in this sacro-idyllic context is the semicircular exedra, used as a seat,[22] with lion's-paw feet visible left and right between the figures. Not even the sundial atop a high column can be taken to indicate a specific place. Such constructions, serving as the tomb and resting-place or votive monument of a wealthy man, could be found in gardens and streets throughout the ancient world, as in the Forum Triangulare in Pompeii.[23] Here it serves rather as a casual and poetic designation of a shady, peaceful place.

The sundial might plausibly be taken to be an allusion to the philosophical event depicted, but it does not necessarily have this

---

[19] A. von Salis, *Altar von Pergamon* 139. Helbig-Amelung *op. cit.* 462. Rostovtzeff, *RömMitt* 26 (1911) 49.

[20] Rostovtzeff, *op. cit.* fig. 13, stucco in the Farnesina, and fig. 18, corresponding gate from Pompeii. Schober, *Wiener Jb.* 2 (1923) 48, Pompeji. Cf. Petersen, *RömMitt* 12 (1897) 329; Sogliano, *MonAnt op. cit.* 405.

[21] Rostovtzeff, *op. cit.* 133 and fig. 61. Diels, *AA* (1898) 120.

[22] Rostovtzeff, *op. cit.* 128, *Schola und Exedra in der Architekturmalerei.*

[23] Petersen already mentioned, *CIL* 10, no. 831: *RömMitt* 12 (1897) 329. Cf. Sogliano *MonAnt op. cit.* 407. For form of sundial, Elderkin, *op. cit.* 92.

meaning. As long as the date of the original composition is unknown,[24] we cannot be certain whether all these objects belonged
to it, or whether they are additions taken from Roman landscape
paintings, or later interpretations. Without them the figures would
seem larger and the whole picture more commanding. The square
format of the Roman copy, employed for a decorative purpose,
does not give any exact indication about the picture's original
shape.

Still, it is certain that this group of seven people reflects a distinguished composition. It is the representation of a conversation—
or rather of a stirring moment in such a conversation—that dissolves
the simple gathering into animated groups, or to be more precise,
into different grades of immediate reaction to an event in which all
the figures participate. Thus we sense the animation at once as our
eyes travel around the semicircle of the composition, even though
not much happens that is visible.[25] The climate of Hellenistic knowledge and description of human nature manifests itself in the disputation among the seven figures, whose outward appearances and
behavior are those of an academic circle of their time. Four sit on
the semicircular bench, while two in long cloaks flank them on
both sides like honorary statues. The one who stands behind the
bench between the sundial and the tree speaks to the pensive-
looking man who sits before him, raising his hand to his bearded
chin. The specific intention is to show the interplay of the participants who seem to converse with one another only casually; it
imparts to the "dotta conversazione" the suddenness of an event
by which this picture differs so much from other similar ones. An
invisible cause shatters the circle, a surprise that affects all and
that each reacts to differently. I cannot fathom why the man with
the diadem—whoever he is—could not have been shown as he is

---

[24] A. von Salis, *op. cit.* 137. The landscape with the exception of some of
its elements, e.g. the exedra, is certainly not early Hellenistic. The corre-
spondence with the Albani mosaic, confirming at least date and sundial, is
also important just as is the antiquated form of the sundial, Elderkin, *loc.
cit.*

[25] Others had the same impression, esp. Helbig-Amelung, *op. cit.* 464,
also Birt, *Alexander loc. cit.*, but I do not agree with their conclusions.

rather than with a scroll in his hands.[26] The latter would cause the picture to lose a point: the seated baldheaded figure, on whose shoulder the standing man rests his right hand, turns toward him, suddenly struck by a word and eager to express his astonishment to his neighbor. The two under the sundial in the background form a similar group. As they lean towards each other, apparently exchanging views, they are at the same time absorbed by something astounding that occurs in their presence. But the man with strangely unkempt hair and beard who sits between the groups is not involved in such a conversation; an aura of respect isolates him. In his right hand he holds a small stick. We do not agree with the opinion of others that he drew figures in the sand with this tool.[27] If that were the case, it would have been easy enough to show the other figures according to the simplest principles of clarity. In any case, the little stick is well known and served both sacred and secular teachers for demonstrations to an audience; we shall list various other examples. It is used by scholarly lecturers, especially astronomers. We learn its ancient name from Vergil: quis fuit alter, descripsit radio totum qui gentibus orbem?[28] Thus, it was called radius, the same instrument wielded so often by Urania, the muse of the stars (Pl. VIII).[29] It was almost always used to point out details on the globe and exactly this is what appears to be happening here too; the unkempt man directs his radius at the large sphere in the foreground. He is the lecturer, and the surprise originates with him; the sphere is the object of his demonstration, which he performs with the help of a radius. The vivid invention of the two listeners opposite him reinforces this impression. The seated one rests his head on the scroll in his right hand, lost in contemplation.

---

[26] Suggested by Birt, *Buchrolle* 103 f.

[27] E.g. Helbig-Amelung, *op. cit.* 463, correctly Petersen, *RömMitt op. cit.* 12 (1897) 330.

[28] Vergil, *Aeneid* 3, 40 f.

[29] Esp. on sarcophagi as here, Pl. VIII. Martianus Capella supplied his Geometry with it imitating her example, radium dextra, altera sphaeram solidam gestitantem, 6, 580. The philosophy of Boethius, *Cons. Philos. I, Prosa* 4, 3 uses the same radius, not to be called a pair of compasses as e.g. in the translation by E. Gotheim (Berlin, 1932) 15. Its size changes, cf. examples below; the one on the mosaic in Naples is not unusual which silenced even Lippold's doubts, *Griechische Porträtstatuen* 73.

I do not agree with the opinion that the standing man with a scroll steps out to the right.[30] Starting back, he reveals by the briskness of his fiery temperament his instantaneous amazement; nevertheless, his proper, well-trained bearing expresses the same intellectual self-confidence as does, in large-scale sculpture, the Lateran Sophocles. Later Hellenism produced many statues in similar standing positions which all derive from a civil canon of movements for the well-bred and cultivated man.

It is not so much a conversation which the momentary gesture represents, but the reaction to a spoken word or an exciting idea. In the same way the agitated groups of Leonardo's "Last Supper" clash like elemental forces, moved by the spoken word, the resonance of which the viewer thinks he still perceives.[31] To this extent an interpretation can be derived from the visual material; but the words which apparently ensued were lost in the destruction of the tradition, while the viewer of the Last Supper is able to add them almost unconsciously because he knows them. In order to rediscover them, we must transfer the inquiry from the formal and visible facts to the intellectual milieu which they represent.

The Albani mosaic does not yield any new information. Although it is much more roughly made than the one in Naples and is even at variance as regards the grouping of the figures, it undoubtedly reflects the same prototype. Only the tree in the background is missing, and the landscape is accentuated by the strange buildings underneath the castle wall that can hardly be ancient in their present state. The sundial on the column, the gate with votive vessels and the exedra are present; therefore they probably are original elements. The man with the diadem and the one who sits next to him form a group similar to the one mentioned above, still recognizable in spite of the modern restorations. The mosaicist caused a confusion only in the next scene when he removed the speaker and placed the pointer in the hand of the figure in the outer

---

[30] Birt, *Buchrolle* 103. I believe even less that as Aristotle, whose withdrawal from the Academy was impending, "he left the gathering in protest," Birt, *Alexander* 296.

[31] Cf. Goethe's famous description of Leonardo da Vinci's "Last Supper" in Mailand, *Weimarer Sophienausgabe* 49, 1, 208 ff.

right corner. He kept the group in the background—the standing and the seated men who converse with each other about the subject at hand—but he changed their form slightly. He replaced the o-mitted or shifted principal person with a seated figure in order to keep a total of seven; this resulted in a most awkward lineup on the right side. He invented the seated figure under the column where-as he rather correctly copied the man with the scroll. By showing him gesturing, he unfortunately spoiled the beautiful invention of the figure with the propped-up head; he also gave him a white himation, handling the colors altogether as he pleased; yet he suc-ceeded on the whole in reproducing the group in a recognizable man-ner. We do not know of course how many phases existed between this version and the prototype, which is certainly more accurately reflected in the mosaic of Torre Annunziata. We can indeed trace the path of transmission up to the Roman gem illustrated by Elderkin.[32] There, however, everybody is silent; the participants are lined up on both sides like heraldic figures and seem to be lost in almost hypnotic contemplation of the sphere which lies among them. It is easy, however, to imagine the old structure of the exedra as part of this arrangement, and the philosopher who sits alone in the background establishes the connection convincingly; the motive of intense meditation, whereby his chin is propped on the right hand and his arm on the knee, proves beyond doubt that he is derived from the corresponding figure in the Naples mosaic. Thus, the gem indicates in its extreme simplification those elements of the originally complex picture which must be considered in-dispensable: the gathering of contemplative men in the exedra, seven in number, and a sphere as the object of their attention. This object always occupies the centre of the foreground. On the gem, the sphere seems to float in mysterious immobility. On the Albani mosaic it is smooth and golden and rests upon a small pedestal which makes it more conspicuous. This pedestal appears elsewhere too; like the radius, it is a tool for demonstrations used in real schools.[33] Thus, the Urania in the peristyle of the House of the

---

[32] Elderkin, op. cit. 102, from Furtwängler, Gemmen 1, pl. 35, 35.
[33] Schlachter, Globus 41 f. It is called the sphairotheke.

Vettii (Pl. IX) has her sphere set upon a similar stone base[34] and with the usual small stick she points to her intellectual domain. Urania, who in accordance with her nature contemplates the movements of the heavens and the stars,[35] can hardly concern herself with any other than the celestial sphere; the sphere's meaning here is therefore beyond any doubt. At the same time she teaches that its earthly didactic image can stand for the infinite universe which is a celestial sphere: thus, the Urania of the House of the Vettii becomes a muse of epistemology and wisdom. The delicate parallel lines that crisscross her globe do not belong to the natural celestial sphere but are meant to facilitate study: they only stand for sketchily indicated circles of the heavens or the orbits of stars.[36] The artist of the Naples mosaic found it equally necessary to characterize the sphere in his picture in a recognizable manner; we gain information from it, although it is by no means certain whether the original was so accommodating to the viewer. The artist covered it with a network of meridians and parallels like a device for astronomical studies.[37] At the same time he placed the sphere on a little box, so it would not roll away; only three quarters of it are visible. The tripod-like container of the Monnus mosaic in Trier on which Arat, advised by Urania, pursues his studies,[38] was arranged in the same way.

The globe shown in the Isle of Wight mosaic rests on a slightly different frame; a sitting man points at it with the familiar stick[39]

---

[34] Cf. *MonAnt* 8 (1898) 278.

[35] *Urania motusque poli scrutatur et astra*, Ausonius, opuscula, ed. Peiper 412. For general concept of Urania, see above.

[36] Meridians of white wax on the globe of an ancient astronomer, Anonymous I from Maass, *Comm. in Aratum rel.* 95, 21.

[37] It was called Arachne; its inventor was Eudoxus, cf. Schlachter, *op. cit.* 15. There, too, more about the gradual development of meridians which seems to have been completed only in the middle Hellenistic period, *op. cit.* 17. Occasionally on Roman coins of the early Imperial times, e.g. coinage of Carisius, *RömMitt* 49 (1934) 165, very clear on a later one from Paphlagonia, Imhoof-Blumer, *Kleinas. Münzen* 1, pl. 1, 8.

[38] *AD.* (1889), pl. 48; miniature replica *RhMus* 48 (1893) 91 with division of heavens by later traditional crossed bands, cf. Schlachter, *op. cit.* 69.

[39] Th. Morgan, *Romano-British Mosaic Pavements* (London, 1886), pl. 21. I owe the reference to L. Curtius. cf. Rostovtzeff, *op. cit.* 49 note. As stated by Morgan 236 ff. the seated figure has the customary dark beard of a phi-

(Pl. X). Apparently it, together with other instruments of observation, indicates the scholarly profession of the astronomer. On a late-Hellenistic tombstone in the museum at Instanbul (Pl. XI), the sphere appears together with writing materials and the kerykeion of Hermes, the god of writing.[40] Here, the meaning of these objects has been extended to that of tokens of the scholar's profession, like the ones in Faust's study. Again the sphere sits on a square base with squat feet as in the Albani mosaic; in the background on the right leans the radius which here has become a sturdy baculus. The low profiled base with a small sphere in front of or underneath the portrait bust of the deceased, as it occurs on several Roman sarcophagi, was perhaps similar to the one in front of the Urania reproduced above. Gradually it was decoratively transformed and became part of the structure of the bust when its motive was no longer understood.[41] If we seek an original meaning in this context, it would be the same as in the scholarly still-life on the Istanbul tombstone, that is, a professional sign or even in a broader sense a reminiscence of the artistic inclination and occupation of the deceased. Altogether there are many examples of the use and meaning of such globes. The base and the arrangement on the mosaic might be an addition by the copyist as is the little box for scrolls on the mosaic in Naples, which is an even more satisfactory addition to the scholarly inventory. Thus they are an intelligible interpretation of the contemporary tradition and therefore rather important. They also show that at least the mosaicist had an idea about the theme of the conversation that went on among the scholars. He did his best to inform the viewer that the topic under dis-

---

losopher, and is therefore a scholar. Behind him a sundial, on his right an open basin with feet on the floor containing unrecognizable objects. A waterclock of the simplest form, like the Egyptian ones, cf. Schäfer, *AmtlBer* 31 (1909/10) 155 ff.

[40] Arif Müfid, *AA* (1933) 135 f., fig. 20.

[41] F. de Ruyt, sarcophagus in Brussels, *Bulletin des Musées Royaux* 3 (1935) 69 ff. and bibliography n. 3. Here the sphere cannot be the foot of the bust as in other examples of the same class; even then it is unusual and meaningful, just as on the base of the Commodus portrait in the Palazzo dei Conservatori. In this case it originated in the Imperial cosmocrator symbolism, cf. E. Strong, *JRSt* 6 (1916) 35 ff.

cussion was phenomena in the heavens: περὶ κόσμου or περὶ σφαίρας.[42]

This, the most natural representation for any astronomical meeting, nevertheless does not yet explain what was reported here, or why there are seven participants, a detail that was traditional everywhere. On the other hand, we cannot suppose that the Seven Sages conducted astronomical discussions. What the ancients expected of them was something quite different. Like every tradition that originates in the mythical consciousness, it was complex and not without contradictions. Except for Thales, the Seven Sages were never regarded as scholars.[43] They were the oldest witnesses of venerable experience, the half-rustic beginning of Greek natural philosophy; yet they were definitely moralists. Their maxims dealt with state, society and the conduct of the individual who lived in them; they were moral in the widest sense and formulated aphorisms, the collection of which was regarded as their actual testament. This efficaciousness would have been remembered as practical and normative if the mythological connection with the Delphic Apollo had not early on linked it to the mysterious undercurrent of the mantic.[44] The number seven was in itself such an element.[45] Furthermore, from early times its representatives' fictitious contemporaneity became part of the mythical character of this conception although the historical data contradicted it. This is connected to the tendency to establish an interrelation between the personages to evoke the memory of gatherings at one of the famous royal courts of the sixth century B.C. This tradition can be traced to Herodotus.[46] The contest for the famous tripod also implied con-

---

[42] As Sogliano rightly pointed out, *NSc* (1897) 339 and Petersen, *op. cit.* 330.

[43] Ὁ δὲ Δικαίαρχος οὔτε σοφοὺς οὔτε φιλοσόφους φησὶν αὐτοὺς γεγονέναι, συνετοὺς δέ τινας καὶ νομοθετικούς.. Diog. Laertios 1, 40 ff. Diels, *Vorsokratiker*[3] 2, 213. Cf. W. Capelle, *Die Vorsokratiker* 62 ff.

[44] Striking characterization by J. Burckhardt, *Griech. Kulturgeschichte* 3. Complete publication Stähelin-Merian 20, 284 ff. Compilation by Barkowski, *RE* 2A. Contents of aphorisms 2255 ff. I had no access to Wilhelm, *Die Sprache der Sieben Weisen*; cf. *Wiener Anzeiger* (1922), 16; I owe the reference to L. Curtius.

[45] R. Hirzel, *Dialog* 2, 133. *RE* 20, 2247.

[46] L. Edelstein reminded me that Herodotus is related to Ephoros, fragm. 101, Diels, *op. cit.* 213: Croesus is called protector of a gathering of the Seven Sages. He also figures in the fable of the contest, cf. *RE op. cit.* 2251 which

temporaneity and mutual acquaintance. The tripod went from one to the other because it was intended for the wisest and finally was set up in Delphi because none of them would accept it.[47] In that light a discussion among the Seven Sages would have been neither a surprise nor something entirely new as subject for a Greek painting of the fourth century B.C. The series of dialogues, the most famous example of which has become the Banquet of Plutarch, but which does not lack its precursors and successors,[48] rests entirely upon this fiction.

That such things existed is meaningful for the philosophers picture, though it cannot possibly illustrate either Plutarch's or any similar banquet. It is not a banquet that is represented but a schola of scholars. Nevertheless our knowledge of the dialogues enables us to form an opinion about the subject of the conversation among the Seven Sages. It is interesting to examine Plutarch's report which quite seriously repeats the table-talk. When the well-known maxims are mentioned, they take the form of dialogues or of answers to questions. Short stories and sporadic reflections on the state and forms of government are added to enrich the conversation; nevertheless they always are moral propositions on which Plutarch focused his attention. Any exception would be noticed in such a consistent selection of subject matter and indeed one exception can be ascertained: it is the story of the letter allegedly written by the Egyptian king Amasis to Bias.[49] Its content, however, is only loosely connected with its narrative introduction. The whole passage differs from its context in form and in content. Once it is detached from its novella-like disguise, its strange character be-

---

points to the date of the transmission. For the gathering in Delphi, Plato, *Protagoras* 343 a.

[47] *RE* col. 2248. See Schwendemann, *JdI* 36 (1921) 158 ff. Bowls and chalices occur as prizes. Wiersma, *Mnemosyne* 1 (1934) 150 ff. (Separation of various versions of fables).

[48] Hirzel, *op. cit.* 138, discussion of earlier dialogues. Ludus septem Sapientium by Ausonius is a corresponding invention but closer to Gnomic aphorisms. The scholia of an old banquet of the Seven Sages were collected by Laban, cf. Diehl, *Anthologia Lyrica* 2, 190 ff. Wilamowitz, *Textgesch. d. griech. Lyriker* 40, n. 3, and *Hermes* 60 (1925), 300 ff. He dates the original invention to the fifth century B.C.

[49] Hirzel, *op. cit.* 141. Plutarch, *Convivium*, ch. 8/9.

comes apparent. Here, not only the usual practical and ethical reflections are reported, but also fragments of quite different considerations concerning the philosophy of religion. In our inquiry we must carefully examine their relation to the Seven Sages as worthy of note. Amasis asked the Ethiopian king who was so fond of riddles a number of questions; Thales answered them more correctly to general applause. They contain parts of an original set of ideas that was certainly not invented for the banquet. These questions lead us to an older, almost lost invention, a special reading of the riddle of the Seven Sages.[50]

---

[50] For the form of riddles and the hidden meaning of Delphic oracles, W. Schultz, *Rätsel aus dem hell. Kulturkreise* 89 ff.

CHAPTER TWO

A RIDDLE OF THE SEVEN SAGES

We shall have to follow the second version, that is, Thales's answers to the questions, which Plutarch himself regarded as the correct ones. But their true value emerges only when we consider those parts of the whole that appear in still another scholarly context related to Thales, namely his biography by Diogenes Laertius.[1] R. Eisler recognized its significance and examined its wealth of mythical and Orphic elements[2] but we shall give it further consideration. We can identify other fragments of the same series of questions in the Florilegium by Stobaeus and elsewhere, all of which certainly belong here because they are related to Thales. Thus, we are by no means dealing with unessential inventions but with a definite tradition. Its recognizable parts must be examined. Only the compilation of all of them will enable us to comprehend the whole to some extent. The following survey might serve this purpose:

Plutarch, Septem Sapientium convivium cap. 9, 153 C.	Diogenes Laertius, Thales 35.
Τί πρεσβύτατον; Θεός, ἔφη Θαλῆς· ἀγέννητον γάρ ἐστι· τί μέγιστον; τόπος· τἆλλα μὲν γὰρ ὁ κόσμος, τὸν δὲ κόσμον οὗτος περιέχει· τί κάλλιστον; κόσμος·	Πρεσβύτατον τῶν ὄντων θεός· ἀγένητον γάρ· Κάλλιστον κόσμος· ποίημα γὰρ θεοῦ. Μέγιστον τόπος· ἄπαντα γὰρ χωρεῖ· Τάχιστον νοῦς· διὰ παντὸς γὰρ τρέχει· Ἰσχυρότατον ἀνάγκη· κρατεῖ

---

[1] *Vitae* 1, 35 ff. The connection with the riddles of *Sept. Sap. Conv.* was recognized early. I owe the following references to L. Deubner: *Diog. ed. Menagius* (1692) 2, 20 col. 2, and Wyttenbach, *Animadv. in Plut.* (1821), *Moral.* 2, 241, which have passed more or less unnoticed. Cf. Zeller, *Philos. d. Griechen*[6] 1, 256, 1. Added by W. Kranz in Diels, *Vorsokratiker*[5] 1, 71.

[2] *Weltenmantel und Himmelszelt* 2, 661 ff. It is to his credit to have recognized here primal elements of the philosophical cosmogony, even though they do not completely establish Thales's authorship. Anyway, the discussion of the unused parallel quotes will lead to a different arrangement depending on the sequence.

πᾶν γὰρ τὸ κατὰ τάξιν τούτου
μέρος ἐστί· τί σοφώτατον;
χρόνος· τὰ μὲν γὰρ εὕρηκεν οὗτος
ἤδη, τὰ δ' εὑρήσει· τί κοινότα-
τον; ἐλπίς· καὶ γὰρ οἷς ἄλλο
μηδέν, αὕτη πάρεστι· τί ὠφε-
λιμώτατον; ἀρετή· καὶ γὰρ τἄλλα
τῷ χρῆσθαι καλῶς ὠφέλιμα ποιεῖ·
τί βλαβερώτατον; κακία· καὶ
γὰρ τὰ χρηστὰ βλάπτει παρα-
γενομένη· τί ἰσχυρότατον;
ἀνάγκη· μόνον γὰρ ἀνίκητον· τί
ῥᾷστον; τὸ κατὰ φύσιν, ἐπεὶ
πρὸς ἡδονάς γε πολλάκις ἀπα-
γορεύουσιν.

γὰρ πάντων· Σοφώτατον χρό-
νος· ἀνευρίσκει γὰρ πάντα . . . . .
[36] Ἐρωτηθεὶς . . . τί ἥδιστον;
τὸ ἐπιτυγχάνειν· Τί τὸ θεῖον; τὸ
μήτε ἀρχὴν ἔχον μήτε τελευτήν·

Stobaeus, Eclog.
I, I, 29 a. Θαλῆς ἐρωτηθείς, τί
πρεσβύτατον τῶν ὄντων· ἀπεκρί-
νατο· θεός, ἀγένητον γάρ·
I, 4, 7 a. Θαλῆς ἐρωτηθείς, τί
ἰσχυρότατον; εἶπεν· ἀνάγκη,
κρατεῖ γὰρ πάντων·
I, 8, 40 a. Θαλῆς ἐρωτηθείς, τί
σοφώτατον; <ἔφη,> χρόνος, ἀνευρίσκει γὰρ τὰ πάντα·
I, 18, I e. Θαλῆς ἐρωτηθείς, τί τὸ
μέγιστον; ἔφησε· τόπος, τἄλλα
μὲν γὰρ ὁ κόσμος, τὸν δὲ κόσμον
οὗτος περιέχει·

Various passages.
Hippolytos, Refutatio I, I, 3.
<Θαλῆς ἔφη> θεὸν δὲ τοῦτ' εἶναι,
τὸ μήτε ἀρχὴν μήτε τελευτὴν ἔχον.
Parallel passages in Diels, Doxographi Graeci 555.

The passage from Plutarch has been quoted in its entirety and
does not need any interpretation for the time being. The omission
from the end of Chapter 35 in Diogenes Laertius is justified because the form of the apophthegm changes conspicuously into that
of an anecdote. The following story about the equal worth of life
and death does not belong here; Capelle has proved that it originated

in a different connection, in a collection of witticisms of the Cynics.[3]
Therefore it should be read as an inter as should the succeeding
anecdotes. The relationship of the above sentences to the corresponding ones of the banquet becomes even more apparent; hence
it follows without any doubt that they are part of the same context.
Each time the essential thing is a list of concepts which are to be
described by related superlatives; Plutarch accomplished this in
the form of a question, while Diogenes Laertius quoted Thales's
words an as *acute dictum*. Nevertheless, the succeeding concept is—
as it were—first logically ascertained by the preceding adjective.
Thus, the character of proverbial wisdom being intrinsically related
to riddles, it adheres to the aphorisms as well as to the questions.
In both cases the first three superlatives correspond to the matching
concepts to be interpreted as answers. In Plutarch and in the Vita
of Thales the oldest, the greatest and the most beautiful[4] are
synonymous with the concepts of god, world and space. A reason is
briefly stated and in two of these three statements it is consistent,
if not literally then at least in content. We shall postpone discussion
of why there is a discrepancy in the argument about the question
of "the most beautiful".

There now emerges the nature of the presumptive prototype
reflected in parts of both fragments. It was a series of superlative
questions or superlative maxims that from the beginning belonged
to Greek philosophy. Here we must refer to the most valuable
distinction made by Iamblichus[5] who lists three ways to formulate
philosophical maxims, the first being τί ἐστιν σημαίνει, the second,
τί μάλιστα. The latter is said to be somewhat later[6] than the
method of the Seven Sages which would apply here but definitely not to the Delphic oracles. However, these three questions

---

[3] *GGA* 176 (1914) 248, cf. Diels, *op. cit.* The following question about the
age of day and night is included by Eisler, *op. cit.* It is, however, at least
formally, an alien element. Therefore his suggested reconstruction is better
left out of the discussion.

[4] Somewhat different sequence in the Vita of Thales, because oldest is directly followed by the most beautiful, and then by the largest.

[5] *Vita Pythag.* 82 ff.

[6] Iamblichus, *op. cit.* 83.

did not complete the series.[7] Plutarch immediately added a fourth
about the wisest which is found in the concept of time. This is
confirmed by the Vita of Thales a few lines farther on; only the
order is slightly altered. Otherwise there is general agreement with
the same reasoning. Finally, one discovers in Diogenes Laertius the
concept of necessity preceding that of the most beautiful and
considered to be the strongest; in Plutarch it is to be found supported by appropriate evidence among somewhat different material.
Therefore it can be stated that five such superlatives which occur
in both places are elements of a common prototype; sounding alike,
they are broken up into coordinated concepts and are given equal
substantiations.

The concepts themselves reveal significant points in common.
God, world, space and time in like manner all stand outside of the
ethical and practical world with which the Seven Sages Philosophy
deals as a rule, and even Ananke[8] is, as a worldly force, fundamentally super-moral. The sequence which emerges as the common
original from comparison of the two testimonies was a compilation
not of ethical but cosmological concepts; this confirms a foreignness
noted earlier of its single parts as they appear in their accidental
context.[9] Above all it shows that Plutarch's redaction was not
intended to be a pure version of the tradition but rather a literary
adaptation. Furthermore it is conspicuously combined with similar
questions of superlatives about objects from the familiar repertory
of moral ideas such as hope, virtue, the most beneficial, or the
most harmful. This is not the place, however, to judge the value
of such aphorisms which certainly also date from earlier times
but to notice that exactly these passages do not occur in both
places but only in Plutarch; therefore they must be regarded as his
additions. On the other hand, one among the five aphorisms by
Thales which are twice attested is quoted by Diogenes but is missing
in Plutarch. Therein the intellect is designated as the swiftest

---

[7] Whether the form of the question or aphorism is original cannot be discussed here, but it seems to have been regarded as venerable. Therefore it is
suitable for the beginning of Pindar's *Ol. I.*

[8] General definition Gundel, *Beiträge z. Entwicklungsgesch. d. Begriffe
Ananke und Heimarmene* (Giessen, 1914); also below 36.

[9] Eisler, *op. cit.* 662.

because it permeates the universe. The explanation given suffices to indicate the cosmological significance because it refers to Nous that rules the universe or rules in everything, a cosmic intellect.[10] It will therefore be necessary to include it in the original sequence in spite of its isolation, so that in Diogenes Laertius we find a complete series of six related theses, a respectable transmission. At this point the hitherto well-established context is lost amid the above-mentioned anecdotes which certainly form a digression. A little further on, the question unexpectedly reappears in a moralizing tone that even Plutarch perceived as irrelevant: What is the most pleasing? The question has to be eliminated from the context, all the more because it is isolated. It is not so easy to decide in the following case where the divine is defined as that which has no beginning or end. The grammatical structure differs from the one hitherto observed: a superlative is not presented and the answer does not consist of a single noun. Nevertheless it is difficult to separate this analogy from the cosmological sequence because it does not belong in the moralizing category. Moreover, the divine as a concept is likely to be expressed by a superlative and the answer follows the first question so directly that it appears to be its natural continuation, or rather to be the end that meets the beginning.

We shall not concern ourselves with each theory about the restoration of the text, but we must at least make an attempt to add this to the complete sequence established above, thereby obtaining the following chain of seven links as a result of the comparison of all traditions:

Πρεσβύτατον	θεός
Κάλλιστον	κόσμος
Μέγιστον	τόπος
Τάχιστον	νοῦς
Ἰσχυρότατον	ἀνάγκη
Σοφώτατον	χρόνος
Θεῖον	τὸ μήτε ἀρχὴν ἔχον μήτε τελευτήν.

---

[10] Also otherwise it is credited to Thales but not quite justifiably. Zeller, *op. cit.* 263.

Having followed the trail thus far, we see the entire structure strangely emerging from its background, and its chief merit seems to be that it contains a seemingly ancient cosmological systematics introduced into the disputation of the Seven Sages[11] through the mouth of Thales.[12] The examination of each individual part will confirm that the whole we have thus gained must have had an additional inner connection which is not superficially apparent.

I. Θεῖον, τὸ μήτε ἀρχὴν ἔχον μήτε τελευτήν: The maxim stating that the divine is that which has no beginning or end can certainly not be viewed as definitive in this form, since its proposition does not achieve a complete description of the divine. It reflects but one of its characteristics, namely its eternity; this quality acquires a certain transparency in the moment that one remembers it is not necessarily applicable to the divine in this formulation, and also that it was never exclusively applied to it. For what thing has neither beginning nor end? There is another answer to this question which differs from the one given by Thales but is no less interesting. It refers to the qualities of the sphere, the mathematical definition of which does not include its lack of a beginning or its infinitude[13] for these are not required for its primary description, although they are directly dependent on it. This is revealed in the instant that one asks where a spherical body begins. Its surface is determined by the equal distance from the centre of all its points so that no distinction exists between them. This is a central philosophical question and for the Greeks a problem of ἀρχή, one origin of their epistemology of the world.[14] Hence the thesis of the sphere as having neither beginning nor end has gained preeminence here. We may call it a formula which, in antiquity and

---

[11] Within the scope of this art-historical and archaeological inquiry, the date of the original of the seven questions, transmitted by Plutarch and the Vita of Thales, cannot be established; they probably originated not in the time of Thales, rather in post-Aristotelian philosophy, cf. below.

[12] He alone was suitable, according to popular thinking, because later his knowledge of cosmic physics was highly exaggerated, cf. Zeller, *op. cit.* 258 ff.; *RE* 5 A, 1210; more details below.

[13] Eukleides, *Elemente* 11, 14/18 (Heiberg).

[14] Also see H. Fränkel, "Parmenides-Studien", *GGN* (1930) 191. K. Sternberg, *Das Problem des Ursprungs in der Philosophie des Altertums*, (Breslau, 1935).

in all European thought that remained in contact with antiquity, on innumerable occasions opened the gates to ideas about supertemporal and everlasting existence. Its importance to philosophy becomes clear in Aristotle's use of it in a place that takes up ideas from Plato's Timaeus with which he disagrees, *De caelo* A 10, 280a 28:[15] "From what has been said, we can infer with certainty that the cosmos is neither created nor perishable, but it is one and eternal, not knowing the beginning and the end of its entire aeons". (Werner Jaeger, *Aristotle*, translated by Richard Robison, Oxford 1934, p. 303) This also informs us about the special application of the formula not to the sphere in general but to the celestial sphere, the πᾶν τοῦ οὐρανοῦ, where it receives, understandably, first priority. This is already the case in the Eleatics and similarly in Parmenides himself,[16] although H. Fränkel has shown that the sphere and its qualities are used there only as an example of "being" rather than as something identical with it.[17] But the beginning of Manilius's didactic poem, Astronomica 1, 211 ff., shows how the subtle meaning of these statements becomes common knowledge, indissoluble from the study of the celestial sphere and the universe:

"Haec aeterna manet divisque simillima forma
Cui neque principium est usquam, nec finis in pisa,
Sed similis toto ore manet perque omnia par est.
Sic stellis glomerata manet mundoque figura."[18]

Meanwhile the same formula had reached the religious and mystic literature where it is sometimes conversely applied, that is, to the divine origin of the world as the beginning and end of all things; in a Hellenistic prayer, for instance, to Isis-Aion, the ἀρχὴ καὶ τέλος

---

[15] W. Jaeger, *Aristotle* 320 f.

[16] For example, Melissos, Diels, *op. cit.* 1, 268, Fragm. 2 and following. See K. Reinhardt, *Parmenides* 211.

[17] Diels, *op. cit.* 236, Fragm. 8, 16 ff. and comparison with sphere 42 ff. Truth also is well-rounded there, Fragm. 1, 29. Fränkel, *op. cit.* 190 f. H. G. Gadamer, *Gnomon* 12 (1936) 85.

[18] Ed. Breiter 7. Similar Ocellus Lucanus, *De Universi Nat.* 1, 25: Ἡ τε γὰρ τοῦ σχήματος (sc. des Kosmos) ἰδέα κύκλος, οὗτος δὲ πάντοθεν ἴσος καὶ ὅμοιος, διόπερ ἄναρχος καὶ ἀτελεύτητος. Commentary by R. Harder 85.

is invoked,[19] or in an Orphic hymn to Uranos, the omnipotent
originator who spherically arches around the world.[20] In this way
the concept encompasses physical cosmology and expands into
the domain of pure speculation, that is, mysticism and magic.
A conventional scholastic view develops, the history of which we
cannot discuss here. It persists throughout the Middle Ages: the
most important textbooks accepted the thesis of no beginning or
end. It will often occur following a mathematical explanation of
the sphere, as in Sacrobosco, *De sphaera*,[21] or in Greg. Reisch's
Margarita philosophica.[22] Through magic and alchemy it reached
Balzac[23] in the midst of the onset of the modern world. It has not
yet vanished. E. R. Curtius has traced its afterlife up to Stefan
George and F. Gundolf. One also encounters it in R. Kassner's "Die
Wiederkehr."[24]

2. Πρεσβύτατον Θεός. It is obvious that the first aphorism of
Thales which is at the same time his first question in Plutarch is
closely associated. There, at the end, the essential quality of the
divine is derived from a mathematical quality of the sphere, as we
have just shown, so that the point treated at the beginning of the
series of aphorisms is the same as the end. God is called the oldest
because he is increate and has no beginning. The above mentioned
Orphic hymn made use of the idea that Uranos has no beginning to
designate him as the oldest being; the increate one is also πρεσβυ-

---

[19] Reitzenstein, *Poimandres* 270, 286 ff. See also Eisler's *Orphic Formula*,
op. cit. 663 and 341, 2.

[20] *Orphica*, Hymnus 4, 2 f. (Abel): ἀρχὴ πάντων πάντων τε τελευτή.

[21] The first edition of the *Tractatus de sphaera mundi*, written as early as
1256, is not available to me. I quote from one of the many later ones, Lug-
dunum (1564) 512: "Quod autem caelum sit rotundum, triplex est ratio,
similitudo, commoditas, necessitas. Similitudo, quoniam mundus sensibilis
factus est ad similitudinem mundi archetypi, in quo nec est principium, nec
finis. Unde ad huius similitudinem factus mundus sensibilis, habet formam
rotundam, in quo non est assignare principium, neque finem."

[22] In many editions, cf. the Basel edition of 1517, 7, ch. 4: Facta est enim
mundus sensibilis ad similitudinem et exemplar mundi intellectualis archetypi et ideal mentis divinae: in quo nec principium nec finis. Sicut in figura
spherica.

[23] E. R. Curtius, *Balzac* 48 f.

[24] E. R. Curtius, *op. cit.* R. Kassner's dialogue, *Corona* 5 (1935), 333 ff.
Thomas Mann, *Geschichten Jaacobs* (1933) 162 ff.: "The secret is in the sphere
..." etc.

γενέθλιος.[25] On the one hand, this shows the close terminological connection of both trains of thought; on the other, their Uranic relationship. The spherical quality of the firmament is formally equated with the mythical and personal quality of the oldest god; and out of the two comes eternity, his mystical characteristic. Moreover, the seemingly abstruse, but in this context quite natural and even inevitable, idea of the spherical form of God, arises from it. This was formulated when the concept of the universe as the superior existence was equated with that of the nameless divine which, even as Uranos, was not sufficiently comprehensible. The idea seems to go back to Xenophanes.[26] Consequently, the concept of the new divine being had to unite with the spherical form of the cosmos, as indeed happened. A reference in Cicero gives verbal testimony for it:[27] "Xenophanes assumed that all is one single whole and immovable; this is god, unborn and eternal, his form is spherical". The significance of these sentences for the aphoristic riddle which we have analyzed here becomes surprisingly clear considering that its last assertion relates to its first in exactly the same way as in Xenophanes the "All One" relates to the not-born God. Even the name of God in the singular indicates that we are beyond mythical piety; this again is the philosophical primal god, the first cosmic cause. However, as long as the divine is without beginning and end, that is, spherical, and God is the oldest, that is, "not born and eternal", the Xenophanic equation must prevail, and thus, for the second time Thales is correct in pointing to the sphere in the foreground of the philosophers' mosaic. For we now know that the

---

[25] *Hymn. Orph.* 4, 2 (Abel).

[26] Zeller, *op. cit.* 653 and Aristotle, *Metaph.* 1, 5, 986b, 18: Ξενοφάνης . . . εἰς τὸν ὅλον οὐρανὸν ἀποβλέψας τὸ ἕν εἶναί φησιν τὸν θεόν . . . Diels, *op. cit.* 121, where reference is made to the famous line *op. cit.* Fragm. 23: Εἷς θεὸς . . . Eisler, *Weltenmantel* 2, 663, reminds us of Pherecydes where the eternity of the gods is discussed, Diels, *op. cit.* 47, Fragm. 1, but not the spherical form of the cosmic god. The inner consequence of these formulas shows that Plutarch phrased the question τί πρεσβύτατον almost literally, following Pherecydes. For Xenophanes, see also Eisler, *op. cit.* 689; W. Capelle, *op. cit.* 123, esp. no. 36.

[27] *Acad.* 2, 37, 118. For criticism of this rendition of statements by Xenophanes cf. Ueberweg-Praechter, *Philos. d. Altertums*[11]77; Gilbert, *Gr. Religionsphilos.* 163. Hippolytos, *Philosophumena* 14; Diels, *Doxographi Graeci* 565, 25 ff. on the spherical god of Xenophanes.

eternal and not-born one could indeed be comprehended by the
image of the sphere. He is the god of Ἕν καὶ πᾶν, according to
whose image the world is created,[28] and whom Empedocles called
Sphairos intending to describe with the word "universe" the nature
that is composed of intellectually speculative and mythical-personal
qualities. We find in Macrobius[29] a cognate religious concept, which
is nevertheless anthropomorphic, of the world as the body of the
god Sarapis. Mystic piety incorporates this and the previous idea,
just as does Christianity: St. Benedict saw God as a fiery sphere[30]
and in German mysticism Mechthild von Magdeburg bore witness
to the same: "In what shape did our Lord appear while in the act
of creation? Precisely in the form of a globe and all things were
within God."[31] Reality and appearance fuse in the words of such
descriptions which can remain valid even when the physical image
of the world is transformed into a new metaphysical image of God
but, as image, remains unchanged, as in Cusanus, Doct. Ign. II. 11,
fol. 38, here according to E. Cassirer, Individuum und Kosmos 29:
"Qui igitur est centrum mundi, scilicet Deus benedictus, ille est
centrum terrae et omnium sphaerarum atque omnium quae in
mundo sunt, qui est simul omnium circumferentia infinita." Kepler
explained the sphere as the counterpart of the divine Trinity.[32]
Seuse attempted something similar in his didactic illustration,
made for Elsbeth Stagel, of the Intellect's flowing out and flowing

---

[28] Plato, too, probably had in mind the exemplary form when in the
Timaeus 37 c, the cosmos is called τῶν ἀιδίων θεῶν γεγονὸς ἄγαλμα. See
also Harder, Somnium Scipionis 123, 2. H. Willms, ΕΙΚΩΝ, (Münster, 1935),
9 f. The reason why, according to Willms, op. cit. 30, the eternal paradigm
is not transferred by Plato from cosmology to anthropology, is to preserve
the concept of spherical prototype as opposed to the anthropomorphical
one. The concept that man is the image of God stems from different ideas.
Cf. Wendland, Philos. Schrift über die Vorsehung 8.

[29] Saturn. I, 20, 17; cf. E. Peterson, ΕΙΣ ΘΕΟΣ 267; Gilbert, Griech.
Religionsphilosophie 207.

[30] E. R. Curtius, Balzac loc. cit.

[31] V. Fliessenden Licht 6, 31. Quotation with similar statements about the
spherical or circle-like form of God (Seuse: "Gott ist ein zirkelicher Ring")
Stierling, RepKw. 44 (1924) 281, Gestalt Gottes.

[32] L. Rougier, L'origine astronomique de la croyance Pythagoricienne,
(Cairo, 1933) 20. Speculations on the trinity of the circle whose centre, dia-
meter and periphery coincide in the infinite, in Cusanus; cf. E. Goldbeck,
Der Mensch und sein Weltbild 164 f.

in;[33] there at the beginning the Trinity is depicted as a structure of two concentric circles. Furthermore, the explanation reintroduces the formula of the beginning and the end: "Diz ist der ewigen gotheit wisloses abgruende, das weder anvang hat noch kein ende." (This is the unfathomable abyss of the eternal deity, which has neither beginning nor end.) The famous dictum "Deus est sphaera intelligibilis cuius centrum ubique circumferentia musquam;" which probably goes back to Alain de Lille,[34] seems to have been the intermediary as well as the most important formulation of all these concepts. The successors of Alain were indeed illustrious: Bonaventura, Thomas Aquinas, Meister Eckhart and Seuse; Cusanus, Marsilio Ficino; and finally Rabelais and Pascal.[35] A basically Platonic idea was kept alive thanks to the scholium on the study of the sphere in Sacrobosco's compendium cited above, which made it accessible throughout the Middle Ages in a slightly different yet recognizable version: "Sic concluditur (sc. ab autore) universum ad Dei imitationem factum."[36] In Dante, Paradiso I, 103 ff. there is a corresponding passage:

> Le cose tutte quante
> Hann' ordine tra loro: e questo è forma
> Che l'universo a Dio fa simigliante.

Following this fundamental equation, essentially the same statements are repeated regarding the divine principle as well as— purely mathematically—the sphere or, physically, the cosmos; since they always corroborate one another, we may speak of a mystical allegorizing of physical facts. In Mechthild the mystic we find an immediate verbal suggestion of the wisdom of Gregorius

---

[33] J. Bernhart, *Die philos. Mystik des Mittelalters* 242 ff. and frontispiece, Stierling, *op. cit.* 279.

[34] Huizinga, *Über die Verknüpfung des Poetischen mit dem Theologischen*, Med. Ak. Amsterdam. 74 B (1932) 11 f.; cf. Bernhart, *op. cit.* 134. The same sentence quoted from *Liber XXIV philosophorum*, and literature 261 n. 159.

[35] Afterlife and history of the tradition in Huizinga, *loc. cit.* Albertus Magnus quotes the sentence as being hermetic; Thomas Aquinas after Alain de Lille, quoted *ibid.* p. 12. From the time of Cusanus and Ficino "circulus" replaces "sphera."

[36] *Op. cit.* cf. above note 21. On *similitudo*, see the passage from Timaeus mentioned above, note 28.

Reisch's[37] manual: "Prima autem omnium sphaerarum maxima mundi machina tota dicitur. Ipsa enim in se omnia continet.... omnetale tum simplex tum etiam compositum in ea complectitur. Ideo perfecta est et unica." The special systematics is effective even in this small selection of innumerable possible examples, all of which paraphrase the single issue of intellectually religious contemplation which, according to its principle unnoticeable, leads back to the following aphorism of Thales.

3. Κάλλιστον κόσμος. "The most beautiful is the world because it is God's creation." The commentary is no longer problematic. The spherical shape of the cosmos is self-evident[38] and if its beauty is the catchword given here because "each part in it is regular," as Plutarch's divergent argument implies,[39] that is where one will look for a new quality of the sphere. Plato's Timaeus serves as our basis:[40]

For the being which is expected to comprise all beings, that shape should really be appropriate which comprises within itself all the shapes there are; therefore he [sc. the demiurge of the world] wrought it on his lathe spherical and round, with centre equidistant from extremity in every direction, the figure of all others most perfect and uniform, judging regularity beyond compare more comely than irregularity. Moreover he rounded its outer surface to a perfect smoothness, and that for many reasons.[41]

---

[37] Margarita, *loc. cit.* Of course these thoughts are lacking in Italian Neo-Platonism of the Renaissance, where Ficino was the first to question this; see the Basel edition 1576, 2, 1114, Dionysus the Areopagite: God has latitudo, longitudo, profunditas, alteritas. Latitudo: "Quoniam virtus et praesentia Dei attingit omnia simul atque comprehendit... Deus simile dicitur, quia neque partium in eo diversitas est, neque alias ipse se aliter habet." Or *ibid.* 1115: "Circularis denique motus significat divinam identitatem."

[38] Since Pythagoras cosmos and σφαῖρα are supposedly synonymous with universe, Zeller, *op. cit.* 548, 3; 521, 3.

[39] Above, p. 21.

[40] 33 B. The passage is a condensation, cf. Stenzel, *Gnomon* 10 (1934) 525.

[41] Diogenes Laertius ascribed this idea to Pythagoras, *Pyth.* 35: καὶ τῶν σχημάτων τὸ κάλλιστον σφαῖραν εἶναι τῶν στερεῶν. Cf. L. Rougier, *op. cit.* 19 ff. The later often used pun cosmos (world) = cosmos (ornament) suggested the equation; cf. Scott-Ferguson *Hermetica* 4, 401.

(Translation from *Plato: Timaeus and Critias* translated by A. E. Taylor [London, 1929], pp. 29-30).

Consequently, the sphere is by virtue of its mathematical structure the most perfect body; it is the purest conceivable beauty owing to the uninterrupted uniformity of the parts comprised in its totality, on which the Plutarchian version of the Thales question is probably based; it comprises within itself all other shapes, that is, all regular bodies.[42] This beauty of the cosmic structure is basically what the whole exposition in the first chapter of the Timaeus deals with, and we cannot discuss it in detail; it also becomes evident how the concepts interconnect and how lack of beginning, eternity, divinity, and perfection perpetually replace each other as different qualities of the one and only existence. Therefore, the evidence given for the same phrase reported by Diogenes Laertius in the Vita of Thales, which does not define beauty mathematically but as originating from God's creation, that is from the same principle, is confirmed in the Timaeus, 29a: "... for the work is the most beauteous of things that have come to be, and its make the best of causes. Since this was the manner of the world's coming to be, it is wrought on the model of that which is apprehended by discourse and understanding and is self-same." (Translation by A. E. Taylor) This idea shifts anew to the concept of likeness[43] on which later, in the Christian version, the beauty of the cosmic structure is based, as for instance Augustine, Conf. 11, 4: "Ecce sunt caelum et terra.... Tu ergo, domine, fecisti ea, qui pulcher es; pulchra sunt enim." On reflection we discover that all this ultimately leads back to the same image of the sphere. The same circular movement which the Timaeus refers to as the thought of God is completed here

---

[42] The doctrine that the sphere contains all regular bodies has a distinct mystic connotation in the Pythagorean equation of the bodies with the elements; this results in an allegory of the effect of unity upon multiplicity. The relation of the dodecahedron to the sphere was a secret whose publication by Hippasus was an *asebeia* for which he paid with his life. Cf. Gilbert, *Griech. Religionsphilosophie* 116 ff. and 117, 1. This, and not contemporary censure, might explain Plato's hesitation to communicate it, Timaeus 28 c.

[43] Above, p. 29, and Sacrobosco, *loc. cit.*

(34c).[44] A similar speculation occurs in Goethe's Wahlverwandt-
schaften: " 'Then perhaps I may briefly mention an important
point,' the Captain added, 'namely that this perfectly clear relation
of parts, made possible by the liquid state, always distinguishes
itself by a definite globular shape. The falling water drop is round
. . .' " [45] (Translation from: *Elective Affinities*, tr. by Elisabeth Mayer
[Chicago, 1963], p. 38). This "clear relation" to itself, as a concept
inherent in the perfection of the sphere's image, had already been
morally interpreted earlier by Marcus Aurelius, esp. Meditations
11, 12: σφαῖρα ψυχῆς αὐτοειδής .[46] It was probably the same conceptual image of perfection that led in Origen to the dictum, later
rejected, about the resurrection of the dead in the shape of a sphere[47]
which is indeed the form of the Perfect. *Omnia continet, perfecta et
unica*, as in Reisch, supra, and throughout the Middle Ages and
even later, statements are made everywhere about the machina
mundi; they attest to the extraordinary afterlife of the Timaeus.
Cicero once polemicized against the mystique of the sphere, but
without much success,[48] particularly since he himself repeatedly
advanced like ideas.[49] Similar comments are often to be found in
Italian Neoplatonism, for example, the words that B. Castiglione
characteristically put into the mouth of Cardinal Bembo:[50] "E se
considerate tutte le cose, trovarete che sempre quelle che son bone
ed utili hanno ancora grazia di bellezza. Eccovi il stato di questa
gran machina del mondo, la quale per salute e conservazion d'ogni
cosa creata è stata da Dio fabbricata. Il ciel rotondo ornato di

---

[44] Similarly Ficino, above, note 87.

[45] Weimar edition 20, 49.

[46] Cf. *ibid.* 8, 41; 12, 3.

[47] σφαιροειδῆς. I wish to thank E. Peterson for the information about
this dogmatic controversy. Earlier literature in O. Bardenhewer, *Geschichte d.
altchristl. Literatur*[2] 2, 190; R. Cadion, *La jeunesse d'Origène*, (Paris, 1935),
128. Survival of the spherical image of the soul in mysticism, e.g. H. Liebeschütz, *Das alleg. Weltbild der hl. Hildegard von Bingen*, note on 108 where the
statements are collected.

[48] *Nat. deorum* 1, 10, 24: admirabor eorum tarditatem, qui animantem
immortalem et eundem beatum rotundum esse velint, quod ea forma neget
ullam esse pulchriorem Plato. At mihi vel cylindri vel quadrati... videtur
esse formosior.

[49] E.g. *Timaeus* 5/6.

[50] *Il Cortegiano* 4, 58.

tante stelle...," and just before, "da Dio nasce la belleza ed è come circulo, di cui la bontà è il centro."[51] This was probably the source of the model allegory "La Belleza" in Cesare Ripa's iconology (Pl. XII); she holds a drawing compass and a sphere—the most beautiful body.

4. Μέγιστον τόπος. One has the impression that the next of the aphorisms attributed to Thales tries to give verbal expression to the attributes making space the largest because "it comprises everything." This looks like a transposition, such as happens occasionally, of the Platonic thesis into a universal-spatial concept that would also have been represented with the picture of a full sphere. We may presume that the spherical form was employed for the thus described topos even though Plutarch saw in this a terminological problem which cannot be solved here.[52] According to him the cosmos is what "comprises everything," whereas space comprises even the cosmos. We can hardly trace this explanation to Thales,[53] but it shows that space is here again mentioned as a cosmic datum.

5. Σοφώτατον χρόνος After this, the Chronos question is best inserted here as an analogy: there is an old connection between the concepts of space and time. Eisler has tried to link the two by means of Pythagorean mysticism of numbers.[54] The Pythagorean speculation, which Aristotle took pains to explain although he attacked it, certainly succeeded in acquiring a similar verbal formulation: "The cosmic sphere appeared to them as time because time, like the cosmic sphere, comprises everything."[55] Thus, once again the "omnia continet" reappears, the characteristic of

---

[51] *Ibid.* 57, 8. Cf. Ficino's commentary on the banquet, *op. cit.* 2, 1336: Vultus huius (Dei)... nitor atque gratia... pulchritudo universalis est appellanda. On similar ideas in Kepler, see Rougier, *op. cit.* 20.

[52] The text is reminiscent of Aristotle's discussion of Zeno's aporia, Zeller, *op. cit.* 754 and n. 1. For the relation of space and world in Aristotle, Zeller, *op. cit.*[3] 2, 2, 398, where, corresponding inversely to its finiteness, the world encompasses space. Eisler, *op. cit.* 471, 3 refers to the Talmudic equation of God = space.

[53] Dümmler, *BphW* 14 (1894), 747.

[54] *Ibid.*, 618, 2.

[55] *Phys.* 4, 10, 218a. This and other passages Zeller, *op. cit.* 1, 545 f., esp. Aetius, *Plac.* 1, 21, 1: Πυθαγόρας τὸν χρόνον τὴν σφαῖραν τοῦ περιέχοντος εἶναι. Leisegang, *Die Begriffe der Zeit und Ewigkeit* 25; Diels, *Doxographi* 318.

the sphere this time applied to Chronos. This equation of time with
the sphere has been repeatedly verified so that Zeller even considered the possibility that behind the name Chronos was hidden an old
symbolic name of heaven.[56] From the corresponding passage of
the riddle of the Seven Sages, we can conclude that we must search
for something similar. Supposing that a spherical Chronos would
fit, and ought even to be expected, in the world of concepts to be
established here, still the inquiry that introduced the suggestion
differs widely from the Pythagorean proof. Wisdom, here the attribute of Chronos, cannot be listed as an attribute of the sphere
but rather one within the All, which Chronos must invent, and which
could suggest a cosmic concept. The passage actually needs to be
explained because wisdom is not a characteristic of time either,
and why the attribution was made is difficult to understand.
Behind Chronos as the Wisest, a transvaluation must be hidden
which renders his astonishing significance comprehensible. It can
be discovered. It is inherent in the often proposed—perhaps even
by Pherecydes—equation of Chronos with Kronos[57] who indeed is
father of the universe.[58] For Kronos has an old though very mysterious relationship to wisdom which later enhanced his function as
fateful constellation[59] and made him the planet of the philosophers.[60]
Indeed it has been said, though not often, that he is "the wisest
god who came into being before Zeus, who contains within himself
what he has created, hence he is filled and is pure spirit throughout;"[61] the well-known Platonic interpretation of the word[62]
which is alluded to here had implied this wisdom of Kronos. It is
actually the mythical quality of the primal god but in the specula-

----

[56] *Op. cit.* 546, 1.

[57] *RE* 11, 1986, 8. Known of course to Plutarch, e.g. *De Iside et Osiride*,
ch. 32.

[58] Pindar, *Ol.* 2, 17. He too transferred it to Chronos.

[59] Panofsky-Saxl, *Melencolia* I, for this development with much material,
12 ff.

[60] Proclus, *Comm. in Timaeum* A 11, E; cf. Panofsky-Saxl, *op. cit.*

[61] Plotinus, Enn. 5, 1, 7. The *omnia continet* apparently also appears in
the many references to this utterance, not explainable here, together with an
allegory of Saturn who is replete owing to the fact that he devours his
creatures. Cf. R. Harder, Plotin 1, 121.

[62] Kratylos 396 b. Kronos is explained as the "pure intellect."

tive equation with Chronos it can turn time also into the wisest "which invents everything." Anyone who wanted to understand correctly the Thales aphorism or even deduce it from Plutarch's question had to be aware of this. Only then can one accurately perceive the unknown in the equation, that is, in the Uranic nature of Kronos already added by Plato,[63] and in the cosmic nature of Chronos. There is even a question whether wisdom as a new dogmatic quality of the Whole is the main issue here and its only, indivisible existence hides behind its name like a decipherable code.

6. Τάχιστον νοῦς. This may be the moment to raise the question about the cosmic mind which introduces yet another side of the same comprehensive identity. According to the just mentioned Platonic scheme, the word Kronos itself stood for the "pure spirit". Furthermore there seems to be enough earlier material to support such an explanation. Orpheus was considered to be the legendary originator.[64] A similar equation between Chronos and the world soul is attributed to Pythagoras.[65] Early philosophy regarded Nous mainly as an agile and motive principle,[66] which probably led to the above mentioned formulation in which it is called the swiftest since it fills everything. Thus the text comes closer to the wording employed by the earlier Stoics for the quite similar pneuma which acts as the finest matter of reason that "penetrates and embraces everything."[67] These almost formulaic statements were extraordinarily effective; they reappear throughout the history of religious mysticism even after the image of the sphere, the original subject of this description, ceases to be mentioned, e.g. in Ficino,

---

[63] *Loc. cit.*; he is the son of the spherical Uranus (according to the above-mentioned Orphic Hymn 4) and the firm band itself of the universe, (Hymn 13).

[64] Eisler, *op. cit.* 441 quoted from Damascius, *de princip.* No. 98 (Abel): ἔοικε ὁ 'Ορφεὺς τὸν Κρόνον εἰδὼς νοῦν; consequently they are identical.

[65] Plutarch, *Plat. quest.* H, 4 B. Zeller, *op. cit.* 546, 2.

[66] For the concept of Nous as the universal substance in Xenophanes and Anaxagoras, Gilbert, *Religionsphilosophie* 233 ff.

[67] *Stoic Fragm.* 2, 1051 (Arnim). For concept Ueberweg-Praechter, *op. cit.* 421; on the wording, see again the statements about Kronos-Chronos. Cf. also Macrobius, Sat. 1, 19, 9 in another context: "summa autem est velocitas mentis."

Dialogus inter Deum et animam theologicus,[68] where God explains himself: "I fill and penetrate and contain heaven and earth. I fill and am not filled, because I am fullness itself. I penetrate and am not penetrated... I contain and am not contained."[69] Zeller has shifted a statement by Stobaeus into the same category of ideas, whereby Thales himself understood Nous in the universe as God.[70] This establishes the connection with the ever implicit idea of the philosophical universal God who, with the universal presence of Nous, now acquires a fifth quality or a new dimension. But simultaneously—and that is what matters most here—the conceivability of this concept (Nous) automatically enters into the image of the cosmos and they become identical; in other words, the sphere appears again, that image which Thales points to and in which the overall symmetrical presence is most purely fulfilled. There is no other image of the spirit.

7. Ἰσχυρότατον ἀνάγκη. "The Strongest is Necessity because it governs all things." It becomes clear from this context that in the following statement—the sixth and last before the synoptic definition, discussed above, of the Divine as the supreme existence— Ananke must above all be regarded as cosmic force, that is as the ruling law in the universe; thus, according to the previous analogies, the super-personal, cosmic significance of "the All" ruled by Ananke as well, can be accepted as certain.[71] It represents in the universe the inviolability of cause and effect and does so as dual essence, as a mythical personage belonging to the oldest theogony or as earliest philosophical concept of the mechanics of natural events. The two fuse and need not be separated here; but we must also state that the mythical figure was never entirely accepted in the religion

---

[68] *The Letters of Marsilio Ficino I*, p. 36. Shepheard-Walwin (London 1975).

[69] Here from E. Cassirer, *op. cit.* 201.

[70] *Ecl.* I, 1, 29 b, Θαλῆς νοῦν τοῦ κόσμου τὸν θεόν, interpreted by Zeller, *op. cit.* 263 f. as a post-Aristotelian addition. For the Philolaus fragment about the world soul, which also penetrates as it surrounds, and its date, see E. Frank, *Plato und die sog. Pythagoreer* 282 ff.

[71] Likewise Gundel, *Beiträge zur Entwicklungsgeschichte der Begriffe Ananke und Heimarmene* 6 f.; the Thales Apophthegm is discussed here according to Diogenes Laertius' and Stobaeus' transmissions.

proper, the rites of the faith. Ananke remained an elusive outsider, often perceived as cruel.[72] But it is important that at an early stage religious and philosophical speculation closely linked Ananke to the elements of the world's existence (among which Goethe included her too).[73] Like the intellect, Ananke is said to be a highly refined, non-corporeal substance which penetrates the whole world and touches its boundaries.[74] Altogether she is a force belonging to the extremities of the world; like Pythagoras' Chronos she is the outermost layer of the sphere,[75] encircling the cosmos[76] or being the farthest vault of the heavens.[77] The complete identity of her nature shines through the variously established but actually transparent concepts. She may be ethereal for the same reason that she is occasionally even equated with the ether[78]—the world soul and supreme element—thereby becoming associated with the concept of the immaterial and the omnipresent which fills the world as the divine primal substance.[79] We may quote here, as Gundel did, Empedocles's cosmic law that "spreads all over the wide-ruling ether"[80] and which, therefore, must have had the same place and function in the universe. Finally one can apply here the universal

---

[72] Gundel, *op. cit.* 29. *RE* I, 2057. Wilamowitz, *Glaube der Hellenen* I, 361. L. Deubner, *ML* s.v. Personifikationen 2090. An express reference to her non-religious quality is to be found in Euripides, *Alcestis* 962 ff.

[73] *Urworte-Orphisch*, III. Cf. K. Borinski, *Philologus* 69 (1910) 1 ff.

[74] Eisler, *op. cit.* 390 f. The Stoics, especially Zeno, incorporated similar ideas, Gundel, *op. cit.* 63.

[75] Above, note 105. Aetios, *Plac.* I, 21, 1.

[76] Again in Pythagoras, who said: Ἀνάγκην ... περικεῖσθαι τῷ κόσμῳ, *op. cit. Plac.* I, 25, 2. Cf. Gundel, *op. cit.* 20; Zeller, *op. cit.* 542, 2. This results in an almost complete equation of Chronos and Ananke, at least in Orphic circles. Cf. Eisler, *op. cit.* 391 and Gundel, *op. cit.* 26.

[77] Τὴν ἀνάγκην οἱ θεολόγοι τῇ τοῦ παντὸς οὐρανοῦ ἐξωτάτῃ ἄντυγι ἐπηχοῦσι; Iamblichus, *Theol. Arithm.* 60 (de Falco) and Zeller, *op. cit.* 542; Pfeiffer, "Stud. zum antiken Sternglauben," *Stoicheia* 2, 112, for the significance of ἄντυξ = sphere.

[78] Eisler, *op. cit.* 415, 4 with reference to Proclus in Plato, *Republic* 2 109 (Kroll). The theology of Aion had a parallel development in many literal reminiscences. Cf. M. Zepf, *ARW* 25, (1927) 288 ff.

[79] Aetios, *Plac.* I, 28, 1; cf. Diels, *Doxographie* 323 and *Vorsokratiker* 145, 8: Ἡράκλειτος οὐσίαν εἱμαρμένης ἀπεφαίνετο λόγον τὸν διὰ οὐσίας τοῦ παντὸς διήκοντα· αὕτη δ'ἐστὶ τὸ αἰθέριον σῶμα, σπέρμα τῆς τοῦ παντὸς γενέσεως ...

[80] Diels, *Vorsokratiker* 366. Empedocles, fragm. 135.

formula of the beginning, middle and end of all things[81] being nothing other than a variant of the formula of the sphere; however, this expresses the creator of being, instead of being itself. Hence Ananke belongs here as the goddess of wisdom, as Aeschylus called her;[82] for the same reason the inner logic of the entire train of thought ends with her. Finally the question is posed about the divine, the sphere itself, and thus the chain comes to an end, forming a perfect ring. It seems to be good archaic terminology, perhaps not without relation to other, mythical aspects of the idea, that Necessity stands for the Strongest, since domination is ascribed to her as to an old goddess of the universe.[83] In the image of the sphere, where the true existence of thought can alone recognize itself, the noncorporeal Ananke becomes conceivable, being the law that forms the world and holds it together. The entire cosmos, as it were, becomes her image and attribute, and Thales in pointing to her poses a question and simultaneously gives the answer.

To draw a conclusion is no longer difficult, because once one has explained the entire chain of riddles, the so-called philosophers mosaic which is the actual subject of this inquiry becomes intelligible at once. Indeed, the figures represented are the Seven Sages and their conversation περὶ σφαίρας is revealed. They do not converse as astronomers but as philosophers whose task as Sages is to come to know the world. The mountain in the background must

---

[81] Proclus, *op. cit.* 345, Eisler, *op. cit.* 415, 5; application of Epicles, is πρώτη, μέση, τελευταῖα in Mithraic theology, Cumont, *Textes et Mon.* 2, 82.

[82] *Prometheus* 936: Οἱ προσκυνοῦντες τὴν Ἀδράστειαν σοφοί. Eisler, *op, cit.* 663, 5 and Euripides, *Helena* 513 f.: σοφῶν δ'ἔπος δεινῆς Ἀνάγκης οὐδὲν ἰσχύειν πλέον; cf. Eisler, *op. cit.* 662, 1. Wilamowitz, *Homer. Untersuchungen* 224, 22, already quoted this verse about the Thales aphorism and made reference to the Seven Sages. Plato, *Politeia* 451 a, refers to the Aeschylus verse: προσκυνῶ δὲ Ἀδράστειαν, ὦ Γλαύκων. Reminiscences in emperor cult: τί θεός; τὸ κρατοῦν etc. Bilabel, *Philologus* 80 (1925) 339 ff. (Heidelberg Papyrus). E. Peterson, ΕΙΣ ΘΕΟΣ 173.

[83] Cf. above with verse from Euripides, *Alcestis* 965: Κρεῖσσον οὐδὲν ἀνάγκας; she is already κρατερή in Parmenides, the all-encompassing band of being wherein the spherical concept is again conveyed. Diels, *op. cit.* 237, 30; Fränkel, *op. cit.* 160. The phraseology in Simonides, Fr. 5, 21, is mythical: "even the gods fight in vain against her.: Cf. Gundel, *op. cit.* 33.

be Acrocorinth, not the Acropolis of Athens.[84] Incidentally, the only sanctuary of Ananke known to us, which characteristically she shared with Bia, was near Acrocorinth.[85] The man on the left with the royal regalia is the tyrant Periander with whom the others have assembled, as at Plutarch's banquet. The speaker with the stick is Thales; he pronounces the prodigious words, the effect of which has long been visible. Now we have discovered what they are: in this circle they can only refer to the image of the sphere.

The painting to which everything goes back was probably based, as von Salis has shown,[86] on an already existing type depicting a gathering of scholars. Its compositional idea was the presentation of a group sitting in a semicircle facing the viewer. The rounded line seems to rise into the picture. This invention, which emphasizes all the characters as well as the sphere, is possible beginning with early Hellenistic art. How old the invention of Thales' riddle is cannot be determined here for it would require its own philosophic and historical inquiry. Nevertheless, it is certain that each aphorism has to do with fundamental ideas of Greek thought; furthermore, Thales is always named as author; thus the compilation, even though it may not be really old, at least suggests a special archaizing tendency. The questions are genuine riddles and the whole a truly meaningful, interrelated structure[87]—only half there, though, as long as the complete picture is not in full view. This reference, taken up and represented by the anonymous painter, is perhaps the most noteworthy. Even if the seven fundamental facts of the philosophical cosmogony proffered here in seven aphorisms or questions exist by themselves and seem to be sufficiently explained, another solution is implicitly concealed behind each of the answers and is equally valid for all of them: they are all intelligible in the image of the sphere and must actually be thus comprehended because only in this image do they gain their most mysterious perfection. Thus the painting came to life in its own hitherto unexplained

---

[84] Likewise G. Lippold, *Griech. Porträtstatuen* 73.

[85] Pausanias 2, 4, 6 and *RE* I, 2057.

[86] *Altar von Pergamon* 134 ff.

[87] Perhaps the total of *seven* questions has an inner meaning, e.g. a connection with the *Seven* Sages.

manner, precisely because it represents the common ideas implicit
and at the same time the true but hidden riddle for the cognoscenti.
Only now the transparency of the concepts is completely revealed,
sequential only in appearance, in actuality contained within one
another. While they appear to form a sequential system, a look at
the painting reminds us that all stages of this course of thought are
essentially identical, or rather they may be brought into a formal
identity; and thus an apparent progression of ideas originates in
play and deeper meaning that should really be called progress
without motion. Everything may be represented with the single
cipher of the one and only comprehensive living primal existence
whether this is the unalterable being in the older sense, or as in the
Stoic formulation, the one divine which, in its various states, is
simply everything that is real.[88] Perhaps the Stoic disguise of this
old idea would correspond even more closely with the date of the
painting; part of the intentions crucial to its artistic design is that
here, picture and word must enter into an indissoluble relationship
of reciprocity and explanation. The riddle, or rather the secret of the
riddle, is shown in a way quite similar to the Telephos frieze, where
the story of the oracle incorporates the meaning of obscure words
into what is representable.[89] The picture is the riddle's true solution.
While it narrates a mythical or anecdotal event, it expands its
original purpose of being informative and legibly narrative, and
begins to transform intellectual events into a transcendent world
which can only be realized in the responsive viewer who is wholly
familar with its symbols. It is no accident that here at the same
time art history acquires a first compendium of symbolic and intellectual references, as whose bearer the image of the sphere is later
entered among the allegories of ancient and post-antique times.

---

[88] Ueberweg-Praechter, *op. cit.* 421; Diog. Laertius 7, 148. Zeller, *op. cit.*
3, 1, 138 ff. Cf. the theological attributes of God, e.g. Reitzenstein, *Iran.
Erlösungs Myst.* 221: God is Aion, Kosmos, Chronos, Genesis. Willms,
EIKΩN 22, epithets of heaven in Plato's *Timaeus*: μέγιστος, ἄριστος,
κάλλιστος, τελεώτατος.

[89] Both inventions prove to be not just formally but thematically related.
In both cases the dispute hinges on a riddle which cannot be represented as
such, as von Salis, *loc. cit.*, has explained also with a view to the Christian
iconography of the scene of the Last Supper.

CHAPTER THREE

THALES

The transformation in a Hellenistic painting of the Seven Sages in colloquy into an aristeia of Thales corresponded to the actualizing narrative style of the period as well as to the status Thales had acquired in the course of time. He was looked upon as the only astronomer among the Seven from early times; however, the gnomic aphorisms play an important role in his tradition, the extensive evidence for which we need not deal with here. Later, he was endowed with a legendary reputation for important inventions;[1] this is supported by the anecdotal element of the aphorisms commented on above. Thales is singled out from the other Sages: he is considered the "First Sage"[2] and wins the famous contest for the title of the wisest, according to at least one of the known versions.[3] These two ideas occur together in a fragment of Callimachus[4] which must represent a good Hellenistic tradition. This is worth considering here since it seems to describe a Thales very like the one in the painting. The son of Bathycles who delivered the prize to Thales found him in the sanctuary of Apollo at Didyma, an old astronomer sketching his calculations in the sand. On being told of the honor bestowed upon him, Thales in annoyance effaced them with his stick; the other hand rose to his disheveled beard in a gesture of contemplation.

One of the limestone figures at the Serapeum in Memphis, whose inscription is lost, seems to have used a gnarled stick in a similar manner for the purpose of drawing or teaching.[5] There is not

---

[1] Apuleius, *Flor.* 18. Diels, *Vorsokratiker* I, 78, no. 109, is one of the most complete enumerations. Cf. W. Capelle, *op. cit.* 6 ff.

[2] Diog. Laertius, I, 22. Diels, *op. cit.* 67.

[3] Cf. above, p. 17. *Mnemosyne* I (1934), 166 ff.

[4] *Pap. Oxyrhynchos* 1011. Pfeiffer, *Callimachi Fragmenta* 43 ff. Diels, *op. cit.* 73 f.

[5] Wilcken, *JdI* 32 (1917) 169 no. 11. For type, cf. the Urania from the Casa dei Vettii, Pl. IX.

enough left of Mariette's drawing to identify the figure as Thales; in fact, it is not even certain that the Seven Sages are represented among the statues of the exedra. An analogous use of the stick merely indicates a similar activity. In general it is not advisable to proceed from the mosaics to the sculptural tradition. In the former, however, a portrait-like distinction between the individual personalities was not only intended but accomplished, especially on the Naples mosaic. However, the renditions are by no means specific enough for the study of single features; the interstices and contours of the mosaic technique discourage close examination. At best one can speak of a general characterization which presents Periander with the royal diadem, his seated companion as bald, the man under the sundial as stocky with short hair, and so on. Within the limits of such a description, Thales is shown as an unkempt old man with a full beard and hair framing his face in a vague outline, single strands not being visible (Pl. V, 1). There might be a curly lock hanging down in the middle of the forehead; otherwise the mane surrounds his face like a nimbus of clouds standing for thick, tangled, perhaps "untended" hair. The wild growth of hair, obscuring his face, distinguishes him from all the others and is used here as his physiognomical characteristic[6] comparable to the Christian iconography for John the Baptist. It is at least an ancient characteristic peculiar to Thales transmitted to us by the mosaic not through verbal but through visual means.

The inscribed herm in the Vatican, unfortunately lacking its head,[7] proves that sculptural portraits of Thales did exist. It belonged to an entire series of portraits of the Seven Sages, of which we know Periander, Bias and perhaps Pittakos.[8] A formal tradition was preserved in the copies of all these portraits. Occasionally they appear in combinations on double herms, which led Visconti to suggest the name of Thales for the head of one such herm in

---

[6] Of course the reason for this characteristic must be the attempt to create the ideal philosopher type, specifically a Cynic; in their circle Thales, the man called first among his contemporaries, was imagined to be dishevelled looking. G. A. Gerhard, *Phoinix von Kolophon* 195.

[7] Vatican, Sala delle Muse 497 a, G. Lippold, *Vatikan Katal.* 20.

[8] Lippold, *Porträtstatuen* 72 f.

the Vatican, but without giving satisfactory reasons.[9] All this makes it more than likely that portraits of Thales and others of the Seven Sages are still preserved in our museums. The head of the double herm in the Vatican, which does not conform to the one with disheveled hair on the mosaic from Torre Annunziata, should no longer be considered a representation of Thales since it is not consistent with the present argument, nor can it offer one of its own. But this does not tell us much, in view of the many existing anonymous portraits of Greeks with long, unkempt, sometimes even wild hair as was typical of the Cynics. To sort out this extensive material we need more evidence; and in fact it is available. Even though in each case the force as evidence is of different value, there is such a strange interlocking in the entirety of the accessible material that we cannot pass over it without comment.

The most important piece of evidence is a head in the Ny-Carlsberg Glyptothek. On the shaft of the herm belonging to it is a palm branch in low relief (Pls. XIII and XIV)[10] which serves as an homage as well as to identify the person represented. The palm branch is obviously the copyist's contribution. F. Poulsen was right to consider[11] it a valuable clue for identification, and we must try to discover its meaning, which was perhaps known to the learned or users of an ancient library. I do disagree, however, with Poulsen's suggestion that the portrait represents Pindar. It lacks all marks of a poet such as a fillet or Dionysiac ivy, more appropriate to Pindar than a palm branch; any such identification, since we have no significant new evidence, must take account of the only existing portrait, however modest it may be. The statue of Pindar as it is reproduced in the Mariette drawing[12] gives us reliable information

---

[9] Vatican, Galleria Geografica 18. J. J. Bernouilli, *Griech. Ikon*, I, 47 f. The relation of the other head to the well-known Bias is certain.

[10] NCGlyptothek no. 424. Bought from an art-dealer, *EA* 1191. The strange condition and colour of the stone of head and herm guarantee that they belong together despite the break. Cf. F. Poulsen, below, note 11. He kindly provided photographs.

[11] *From the collection of the NCG* I, (1931) 46.

[12] Pindar from the Exedra of the Serapeum in Memphis, *JdI* 32 (1917) 164. The drawings seem reliable for antiquarian detail, but are undependable for physiognomical detail. No. 9, *loc. cit.* 168 f., closely recalls in bearing and expression the so-called Arat Albani, *ABr* 995/96, although the locks on the shoulders are absent.

about some details such as well-kept, curly hair that falls down to the shoulders, and a credible taenia. The actual portrait has not yet been located; but it is definitely not the herm in Copenhagen and with that, all probability fades that it represents Pindar or any other poet. Moreover, according to the usual logic of copyists, the palm branch would hardly denote a man who composed paeans but rather one who won prizes. Herein lies the real aporia. An athletic contest is out of the question since the portrait represents not an athlete but a thinker, with all the marks of intellectual rather than physical power, the seat of which is the forehead, furrowed by passionate efforts. On the other hand, philosophers do not compete in contests, at least not as thinkers. There were no philosophical contests as such except for a single, famous one which, however, was legendary: the contest of the Seven Sages in which Thales won the prize. He later dedicated this prize to Apollo according to a well-known custom. As soon as one places the herm from Copenhagen within the circle of the Seven Sages, all the hitherto unsolved problems disappear. The palm branch, otherwise hardly an attribute suitable to a scholar, here significantly describes the first among equals, an easily understood, anecdotal reminder like the aphorisms inscribed on the shafts of the Vatican herms. Just as in Callimachus, he is called ἦν γὰρ ἡ νίκη Θάλητος.[13]

An argument is thereby established that compels us to give serious consideration to the physiognomical resemblance between the portrait of Thales in the Naples mosaic and the otherwise puzzlingly fine herm. Under these circumstances one may describe a series of peculiarities among the correspondences with much more confidence than may usually be mustered before objects so difficult to compare. The previously noted portrait feature of dishevelledness is apparent in both and must be further investigated. The tangled hair generously frames the face without actually being long; it reaches down to about the middle of the cheek over the ear. Right underneath are curly sideburns and a goatee, the ὑπήνη of Callimachus; together they form a cloudlike foil around the face, on the marble head exactly as on the mosaic. The shape and con-

---

[13] *Loc. cit.*

tours of the face are similar; even the rolled-up curl hanging down
the middle of the forehead, a sculptural motive peculiar to this
invention, is present. As far as the comparison can be carried out,
it entirely corroborates the identification permitted by the interpretation of the palm branch. Both monuments represent Thales,
both possess the same portrait conceits, and, therefore, both belong,
although at quite different places, within the development of the
same pictorial tradition, the origin of which was an imaginary
portrait of the late fourth century B.C., perhaps one from a famous
series of portraits of the Seven Sages.

We already have a compilation and critical analysis of the
existing copies. F. Poulsen has rightly called the copy in Petworth
House the best replica, and it will be here listed first:

1. Petworth head, M. Wyndham, *Catalogue of the Coll. of Lord
   Leconfield*, p. 53 f., pl. 30.
2. Copenhagen, Ny-Carlsberg Glyptothek No. 424. The copy discussed above.
3. Wilanòw. J. Starczuk, *Sculptures antiques de Wilanòw*, Pl. 9,
   No. 10, p. 418 ff. Listed erroneously as "unknown Roman."
   Added to the list of replicas by G. Lippold, *Gnomon* 10, 1934, 238.
4. Florence, Uffizi. *ABr* 617/618.
5. Rome, Museo Capitolino, Stanza dei Filosofi 71. *ABr* 613/14.
6. Rome, Museo Nazionale delle Terme. Here, Pls. XV and XVI,
   from Negative 8082 of the German Archaeological Institute in
   Rome. Added to the list of replicas by G. Lippold, *op. cit.*[14]

The considerable variation in the copies is obvious. 1. The
Petworth head displays typical features of a portrait of about the
time of Lysippus;[15] the face is oblong, the curly hair long and

---

[14] Freiburg i. Br. University Collection, mentioned by P. Arndt in Lippold,
op. cit., but out of place here. Figured in *Katalog Helbing* (Munich, October
1914), Pl. 1, no. 13, and *Helbing* (June, 1914), Pl. 10, no. 510. Cf. *EA* 1643/45.

[15] The original was probably in bronze, the execution of details similar to
the bronze satyr from Olympia, which E. Schmidt suggested to be the one
by Silanion, *JdI* 49 (1934), 193 ff. In the Petworth head, the beard, otherwise
quite schematically treated by the copyists, has preserved some features of
the original. Comparison is instructive for the treatment of details by
copyists; only the most characteristic traits are retained.

profuse on the sides. Long tufts of hair cover the forehead; in the centre between them appears a question-mark shaped lock. 2. Copenhagen: the structure is similar though the face is less elongated, the lock in the middle of the forehead more isolated. 3. Wilanòw: badly damaged Antonine copy; the head is more oval; the centre lock is part of dense curling. 4. Florence: the shape of the face is well preserved. The unkemptness is much emphasized, especially above the forehead, but generalized motives replace the centre lock. 5. Capitoline Museum: the form of the face is more oval, the hair less abundant. The profile displays clear motives of curls. The forehead is less furrowed, the brows not so intensely contracted. 6. Terme: special attention is given to the expressive features of this face, for this series unusually Hellenistic looking; it is emphasized by a definitely Hellenizing hair style which a copyist seems to have arbitrarily added, since the other copies do not have it. The face is oval which makes the forehead look different. The lock in the middle is different too, hanging deep down over the forehead.

On the whole one can say that in spite of considerable alterations by the copyists the series is coherent and transmits consistently a specific invention. Its Thales expresses the passion of thinking. A strongly built face, deep-set eyes and clearly marked brows intensely contracted over the nose are characteristic for him. The type could be called "the passionate thinker"; the image of the sage that the Cynics had started to develop at the time we date the portrait perhaps influenced its invention.

Besides this series, another slightly less numerous one is preserved that bears a strange relationship to the first, consisting of contradictory similarities and differences. We mean the heads which G. Lippold proposed to call Solon,[16] three of which are known to date:

a) Madrid, Prado, *ABr* 501/2.
b) Rome, Palazzo Altemps: statue alien. *MD* 58. *EA* 2369/70.
c) Rome, Villa Albani: belonging to double-herm. *ABr* 377.
   Bernouilli, Gr. Ikon. I, 43, fig. 5.

---

[16] Lippold, *Porträtstatuen* 71, A.2.

Here again we are dealing with a series of replicas, but they are neither as expressive nor as well preserved. (a) Madrid, the best preserved example, probably dating to the time of Antoninus Pius,[17] is so assimilated to the emperor's portraits that the incorrect labelling is understandable. The face is elongated, the beard rather pointed, the brows conspicuously slanting down at the outer ends. These features produce considerable difference in the expression by comparison with the previous series; the general character is more serene and at the same time less interesting. But the hair style is similar though less curly. The forehead is not square, but rather tapering. The coiled lock hangs carefully isolated in the middle of the forehead. The matted tufts above the ears are rather similar, the sideburns reach down to the middle of the cheeks. Near the eyes the line is not as straight but is rather curved; the soft lines of the Antoninus portraits prevail throughout. In this head there is a peculiarity repeated in (b) Palazzo Altemps, not well preserved but with more authentic details, and we shall see that this singularity will repay careful investigation. The face is still elongated. The angular hairline around the forehead reappears and a closer resemblance to the first type is thereby achieved. The question-mark-shaped lock is clearly set off in the middle of the forehead. The outlines of the eyes and brows are straighter than in (a). The hair, trimmed as if shaven in a straight line at the nape, is the same as in (a), while in the palm branch series the locks are longer over the nape of the neck than over the ears.[18] (c) Albani is on the whole like (b) but (b) has been rather summarily treated. Its merit is that it has a long, uninterrupted connection with the Vatican replica of the Periander portrait; thus in all probability it leads us again to the circle of the Seven Sages, one of whom it must have represented.[19]

[17] E.g. Munich, Glyptothek, *Führer*, Saal XI, no. 32, or Vatican, Museo Chiaramonti, *Amelung* I, 682.

[18] The two heads, discussed by E. Schmidt, *loc. cit.*, as works by Silanion, show the same difference, the so-called Apollodoros (back view in *JdI* 47, 1932, 293) with short hair, the pugilist from Olympia with hair hanging down over the neck.

[19] See above for Periander's portrait. It is interesting that the mosaicist did not employ this invention; Periander standing on the left side is characterized quite differently. The concept of the princely portrait of the Diadochs had crept in, possibly already in the original painting—for the date of which

These are the facts; how can they be interpreted? The first series transmits a portrait of Thales, the second, one of the Seven Sages not yet identified. The two groups are not identical, or even accidental variants of copyists; the second group, though less well preserved, has characteristics which distinguish it from the first. We must assume that it goes back to an independent original. But the two groups share other characteristics, mainly important formal features of the entire arrangement: the longish hair of the unkempt philosopher, and particularly the rolled-up lock on the forehead which is so conspicuous in the copyists' tradition and which connects both groups to the Thales in the mosaic, and to him alone. This is all the more important since it is a question of an ideal portrait, that is, a free invention made up out of just this kind of formal characteristics; whose intention was not to render actual features but to create a personality intelligible in clear physiognomical details. It is hard to believe that for a series of the Seven Sages, consisting of such clearly characterized and distinct images, such similar formal features for two different personalities should have been chosen and that the later tradition, the specific details of which are mostly lost, should have accepted them. But since the differences are so obvious, another solution seems more likely and this is that the unruly-haired fellow with longish hair, high forehead and matted lock represents in both cases, perhaps corresponding to two different prototypes, the same man, Thales, who could easily be brought to mind by such characteristics. If so, we are not dealing with two different portraits but with two versions or phases of the same, one being a passionate, almost choleric type while the other, on the contrary, represents a much quieter, more melancholic temperament without blurring its decisive peculiarities.

What these differences reveal about date and style is difficult to determine, especially considering the poor preservation of the second series. Its prototype is perhaps somewhat earlier, antedating the original of the palm branch series which elaborated it further. One

─────────

this would be important. The seated figure who leans the scroll against his chin might be Bias. The corresponding figures in the two mosaics have some things in common with the herm of the misanthropist in the Vatican, Sala delle Muse 528.

might ask why the tradition of the "choleric" type is so much more homogeneous and numerous than the other one. But such questions would be of use only in a history of the tradition of Greek portraits, specifically those of the fourth century B.C. Here it is sufficient to establish the two variants and to examine their relationship. The fact that there existed among the copyists' resources two such distinct inventions as have been described here that passed as portraits of the same man, comes less as a surprise than as confirmation of previous experience. The two versions show exactly the same relationship between two or more slightly varying works of art which represent a conceptual likeness; it is worth noting that this is the case with almost all famous portraits of this period. Just as well-known variants of the portraits of Socrates or Plato, Sophocles or Euripides existed, so we here recover two versions of the image of Thales, different in origin but similar in concept.

CHAPTER FOUR

WORLD SPINDLE AND CELESTIAL SPHERE

We did not mention Plato's famous account, describing Necessity holding the spindle of the world,[1] when we discussed Thales's question concerning Necessity because this account leads indeed into another world. One has only to call it to mind to perceive at once the beginning of extraordinary developments, combinations and ramifications which the subject of the symbolic image of the universe had already produced with respect to the concept of fate. Plato allotted it the most supreme as well as the most complete affirmation, a classical compilation of all its motives, as will soon be demonstrated in the analysis. With regard to Thales's riddle a strange wealth of imagery unfolds in this account. The riddle presupposes, as do other, basically equivalent, questions, completely abstracting the universal forces into the laws of mathematical categories. Its visual representation as a sphere could either be a real globe meaning the world or a simple hieroglyph standing for thought. Instead, the reader of Plato feels that he is being carried back from philosophical abstraction into the realm of pure mythological storytelling. The goddess of the universe, enthroned above all the spheres with her daughters, the Moirai, appears as a visible, mythical conception which seems almost incompatible with the quite differently formed and demonstrated idea of the riddle, if only because a divine personage would be meaningless outside the universe. If, however, we pose the art-historical question whether this image, which is built up in such an extraordinarily tangible, detailed,[2] and comprehensive way in the poetic version of the description of a real vision, we would fail to find an answer. The image contains inconsistencies which are difficult to reconcile; however, what is even more noteworthy, it is also entirely absent from the pictorial

---

[1] *Republic* 616 B ff.
[2] K. Reinhardt, *Platons Mythen* 108 ff.

narrations of myth preserved to us,[3] and a similar or even equivalent personification of Necessity is not to be found in Greek art to this day. This could be merely accidental, but it does reveal the solitude of Plato's thought which is in striking contrast to any genuine Greek myth. This relationship already hints at the strange intermediate position between abstraction and myth. Platonic thought does not really belong to either category since it is a grandiose fantasy created to interpret the universe and as such plays its role in Platonic philosophy.[4] For this reason it includes figurative elements within the mythical ones, though the image was perhaps never represented as a whole. An inquiry after traces of these elements can indeed be undertaken in art and an iconographical commentary could begin there. One would have to establish how many single pieces of demonstrable artistic imagery this account contains or to what extent it generated pictorial representations. The ancient ideas about the universe and fate actually had their own history of images; of which the hieroglyphic means of expression of the picture of the Seven Sages was an exceptional case, motivated by the peculiar character of the represented story. Their image can be traced back to divine personalities to whom it perhaps belonged from the earliest time. Thus, a new world of meanings in art develops in the intermediate area between abstraction and myth which progressively encompasses forms of pictorial representation, even to the extreme freedom of speculative interpretation of myths and pure allegory.

The actual purpose of the strange journey of the souls is to describe Ananke; Plato has rendered it as an account of the man Er. It is introduced by a short description of what the world looks like from the outside. Although these few sentences seem to be closely connected with the following ones, we must discuss the two passages separately, as images seen from two entirely different points

---

[3] For earlier controversies, see Boeckh, *Kleine Schriften* 3, 297 ff.; also J. Adam, *Republ. of Plato* 2, 441 ff., E. Pfeiffer, "Studien zum antiken Sternglauben," *Stoicheia* 2, 111. A. Rivaud, *Rev. d'histoire de la Philosophie* 2, (1928) 8 ff.

[4] Physics as myth, as explained by E. Hoffmann, "Platonismus und Mystik," *SB Heidelberg* (1935), 2, 94.

of view. Earlier readers of the text were already aware of this,[5]
and it deserves more attention because in both instances a highly
impressive and at the same time memorable sight is meant to be
conveyed. The spherical appearance of the universe is thereby not
explicitly mentioned; nevertheless, it can here be assumed from the
relationship to the similar statements in the Timaeus.[6]

During their journey, the souls gazing down from an unspecified
place[7] discern, extended from above through the heaven and the
earth, a beam of light like a pillar that is compared with the rain-
bow probably on account of its transparency.[8] To this they came
after going forward a day's journey, and they saw there at the
middle of the light the extremities of its fastenings stretched from
heaven; for this light was the girdle of the heavens like the under-
girders of triremes, holding together in like manner the entire
revolving vault.[9]

Most likely this rainbow-like pillar of light is to be understood as
the super-celestial sight of the Milky Way which, in Pythagorean
concepts at least, is conveyed as an outermost circle of fire and the
force surrounding the whole.[10] At any rate, from this passage,
leaving aside the known difficulties of verbal and contextual interpretation,[11] we derive the following: the sky is held together from
the outside by bands as a barrel is by staves. The passage 36 B/C
in the Timaeus should be compared; there, the cosmos is actually

---

[5] Adam, *Republic* 441, 447.

[6] The passages dealt with above.

[7] For the indication of place, Stenzel, *Platon der Erzieher* 181 f.; underworldly and Uranic elements are mixed.

[8] A universal axis of light, for which a correlative in the real universe can
hardly be found. For this problem Boeckh, *op. cit.*, 300. This probably develops the picture of the spindle whose axis passes through the centre of the
world. Adam, *op. cit.* 447. A. Speiser, *Die mathematische Denkweise* 56; an
explanation of a similar aporia between concept and reality appears in
Dante's cosmography.

[9] Translation from: Paul Storey, *Plato, Republic*, Loeb Classical Library.

[10] Already in Cicero's Dream of Scipio, c. 3, cf. Boeckh, *op. cit.* 305; for
interpretation of the whole passage, Adam, *op. cit.* 446 f., and commentary.

[11] Adam, *loc. cit.* Accordingly, the light would pass as imaginary axis of
the universe through its centre and turning round the poles (*loc. cit.* fig. 1)
it would encircle the world as a band; thus, band and axis would be one and
the same in substance.

constructed as a sphere from two such rings, perhaps circles of the heavens like the sidereal equator and the ecliptic.[12] These intersect like the strokes of a chi in the letter forms of the fifth century B.C. If one translates these descriptions into the imagery of the monuments, the result is a well-known sight: it is the picture of the celestial sphere with crossed bands that medieval art took over from Roman antiquity. With a cross attached on top, it was sanctioned as the orb of the Holy Roman Empire.[13] Thus, this significant and much used symbol can claim to illustrate a concept of the heavens already known to Plato, although at first we understood it to be a Hellenistic invention;[14] it was merely transformed by schematic rectangularity of the bands into an ornamental and popularized illustrative shape. The Zodiac and celestial equator, if these are meant,[15] do not intersect perpendicularly but obliquely. Plato's comparison with a chi therefore did not necessarily gainsay the letter forms of his time.[16] On the older and better monuments as on the Urania coins (see fn. 14), the two bands of the sphere are indeed inscribed as oblique circles. The symbolic imagery absorbed the objective-scientific meaning only later. However, the representation of the two bands has always identified the celestial globe in art most comprehensibly, and the Platonic vision has indeed used the heavenly band mainly as an optical element.

---

[12] Esp. A. E. Taylor, *Commentary of Plato's Timaeus*, 146 f. and 160 ff.

[13] For crossed bands, see above; blue globe carried by Apollo as cosmocrator, here Pl. XVII, on fragment of Pompeian wall painting, F. Cumont, *Textes et Monuments* 1, 89 and n. 5. The Mithraic practice shows indeed that this was originally the form of the celestial globe, contrary to G. Rodenwaldt, *AA.* (1931) 332, though further interpretations occur later on. For history of the orb C. A. Böttiger, *Amalthea* 1 (1820) 28 f.; Schlachter, *op. cit.* 69; A. Alföldi, *RömMitt* 50 (1935), 118 ff. The Swedish Riksäpplet, probably from the time of Erik XIV, indicates the new interpretation as terrestial globe by indicating the countries, *Konsthistorisk Tidskrift* 2 (1933) 104 and fig. on p. 97.

[14] Earliest identifiable example: the coins of Uranopolis, esp. *ZNum.* 41 (1931), pl. 5, 2; again we find the celestial globe with the eponymous goddess Urania sitting on it. The date is about 300 B.C., cf. Lederer, *op. cit.* 48.

[15] For meaning E. Pfeiffer, *loc. cit.*; F. Cumont, *loc. cit.* Zodiac and Milky Way? The zodiac occurs often on monuments, the latter never.

[16] A. Kirchhoff, *Stud. z. Geschichte d. griech. Alphabets* (1887) 95.

Zeller[17] already called to mind the terminology employed in earlier Greek philosophy to elucidate the character of Ananke, especially where it followed the Pythagoreans. Ananke—the cohesive force of the outer limits—was also sought, apparently, in the fiery periphery of the cosmos, as she could be the sphere of fixed stars and the outermost layer of the world. In this she resembles the world soul that had been postulated in the Timaeus. In this connection Adam[18] has already pointed out the similarity of wording in the descriptions. Thus, the material seems on the point of allowing the concept to flow back into the hieroglyph of the spherical image of the universe, capable of encompassing everything, and thereby into the stream of those known and untiringly repeated speculations, the course of which we have outlined above. It is significant that this does not happen here. Instead the vision is transferred in a few words beyond the one and only universally rounded and self-sufficient cosmos to the exceedingly surprising sight of Necessity enthroned, spinning just this cosmic globe on her thread.

She is unexpectedly introduced to the reader with hardly any preparation; her outward form remains shadowy, no description of her place is given, nor is any attempt made to describe her presumably enormous size. Only toward the end of the passage (617 B) do we learn that the giant spindle is moving in her lap, hence she is seated. However, the description concentrates first only on this spinning implement which not only symbolizes the single concrete outward appearance of the world but its manifold mobility, the inner mechanism of the great machina mundi. Therefore Ananke cannot be intertwined with it as law, but appears suddenly as principal cause, a primum movens of the whole as divine person.[19] The picture is thereby completely changed. It will change again just as suddenly, when (617 D), derived from a different concept, the same Ananke takes part in the judgment of the dead and the

---

[17] *Ibid.*, I, I, 435, n. 2. For statements about Ananke, see above 40 ff.; for explanation as the sphere of fixed stars, Pfeiffer, *op. cit.* 112. Cf. F. Ettig, "Acheruntica," *Leipziger Studien* 13 (1891) 308.

[18] *Ibid.*, 447, commentary.

[19] Ananke as cosmic cause: Adam, *op. cit.* 452.

election of the souls, whereby a new scene and, optically, a change of dimensions becomes necessary. To understand the passage, it is essential to recognize its metamorphic character. The images flow into each other like the freely shifting scenes of a dream, and, like a genuine dream, they base their unreality in general on separate elements of reality which in return become individually recognizable as historically comprehensible concepts. Such an element is the image of the universe surrounded by bands. Ananke, the spinner who is quite unexpectedly introduced as the cause of their movement, must be seen in a similar light. The transformation of one image into the other is described just before (616 D). The first words seem to continue the context: we learn that Ananke's spindle is attached to the same shaft from which the bands of heaven start whereby our contemplation is suddenly directed upwards and we become simultaneously acquainted with the reasons for the just mentioned rotation of the world. Here now the cosmos has been changed, from one word to another as it were, into a spinning implement[20] which is entirely new. It is indeed that part onto which the thread, weighted by the whorl, is spooled as it emerges from the loose material of the distaff; it is the only movable part. The conclusion one might naturally derive from this image would be that the world is the web of Necessity. Yet this is nowhere stated nor is it what was intended by the Platonic concept. In fact, not the web but the whorls are the subject of the discussion; thus the idea has taken a new turn which is equivalent to a sudden interruption of the hitherto coherent concept. The break, if this is what we may call the interlocking of the visions, happens just in that passage where the discussion of the theory of the spheres begins (616 D).

The metamorphosis of the impersonal image of the cosmos into the mythical personification precedes this and is accordingly its prerequisite, although not its real cause as will be demonstrated momentarily. First we must study the figure of the spinning woman because she creates the predominant, higher idea for all that follows.

---

[20] Ἄτρακτος is here the name for the entire implement as opposed to the shaft (ἠλακάτη) and whorl (σφόνδυλος); characteristically, neither thread nor distaff are mentioned. Boeckh, *loc. cit.* 312. H. Blümner, *Technologie* I, 123 ff.

She represents a fundamentally new *Concetto* which, however, can by no means be called internally homogeneous. It is like a figure in a dark room sporadically illuminated as if by lightning from different sides that fades away forthwith; thus, the never wholly visible figure leaves an impression fed by manifold visions and sudden intuitions; it is dreamlike and thereby all the more impressive. Yet we can perceive this intellectual many-sidedness as the main characteristic of an idea whose poetically mingled elements are at least still partly recognizable as such, in spite of the transformation leaving their traces in the sequence of images.

The Greeks knew the spinner as goddess of fate but called her Moira, also Aisa, not Ananke.[21] She belonged from early times not so much to myth as to poetic tradition, even as early as Homer.[22] The lyric fragment, added by Gundel,[23] has Aisa, exactly like Plato's Ananke, operating an adamant spindle. On the whole she seems to have remained a rather abstract personality whose origin could be easily remembered by her name.[24] However, the plurality of two, three or more Moirai is at home in the myth where they are nymphlike, indistinct beings bearing a striking resemblance even in art to the sisterly groups of Nymphs or Horai. The act of spinning is originally foreign to them,[25] and it is noteworthy that they existed for a long time on monuments without any attributes; their influence is exerted by their magic presence.[26] In Homer Aisa is

---

[21] Earlier literature dealing with her concept W. Gundel, *Beiträge zur Entwicklungsgesch. der Begriffe Ananke und Heimarmene* (Giessen, 1914) 48. Cf. Wilamowitz, *Glaube der Hellenen* 1, 360 ff. The equation Moira = Ananke in Moschion, cf. Gundel, *op. cit.* 39.

[22] *Iliad* 20, 127 f. (Aisa); 24, 209 f., where the Moira is called κραταίη, her typical epithet, see above, p. 36 for Ananke.

[23] Gundel, *op. cit.* 48, n. 8. Stobaeus 1, 5, 11. Perhaps by Simonides, cf. Wilamowitz, *Isyllos* 16 f.

[24] Eitrem, *RE* 15, 2449.

[25] We do not yet know how the image of the spinner was conferred upon any particular one of the Fates; cf. Eitrem, *op. cit.* 2480 and C. Steinbach, *Der Faden der Schicksalsgottheiten* (Diss. Leipzig, 1931) 8 f.

[26] See the François Vase, FR. pl. 1/2 and the black-figured amphora in the Louvre, *MonInst.* 6/7, pl. 56, 2; here the mythical concept is at its purest. The metaphor of spinning seems unknown to these artists; their motive is the echeloned procession. Therefore they are often added to the Horai, e.g. on the Hyakinthos altar at Amyklae, Paus. III, 19, 4. Reinach, *Rép. vases*

once surrounded by the κλῶθες[27] perhaps the combination of fate-goddess and women spinning most similar to the Platonic group, as the name clearly indicates. Moreover, we must consider that all these beings, following an old religious tendency, are always concerned with the individual fate of humans and gods, something that appears only later in Plato's account. On the contrary, his Ananke has indeed a super-individual and superhuman character which already indicates how far removed from this domain his story is, its wealth of references surpassing it; the basic concept is different and though there is often a reminiscence of the concept of the Moirai and a connection with them in poetry and religious belief, we can neither grasp it clearly nor understand it fully from this concept alone.

At this point we shall gain by digressing from our deliberation to examine the monuments. We shall begin with the artistically rather crude representation on an altar in the Capitoline Museum (Pl. XVIII),[28] whose importance for the history of religion has not been sufficiently appreciated. According to its inscription it was dedicated to Dia Suria by a certain P. Acilius Felix. Thus the image on the front side, of which only the face and most of the two lions' heads on the right and left are destroyed, is clearly defined: it represents the object of the dedication, Dea Syria, richly furnished with attributes and enthroned in the hieratic frontality of a cult image between her two animals. This must have been intended to call to mind the large image of the goddess in the mother temple at Hierapolis-Bambyke; it completely corresponds to Lucian's description of the arrangement of that cult image between the lions.[29] The Hellenistic version,[30] though artistically rather poor, renders it

---

I, 468, must be deleted; it is one of the many pictures of women in everyday life. The potsherd from Ruvo, Preller-Robert, *Griech. Myth.* I, 533, possessed, according to the inscription, several Moirai. The Kerch fragment, R. Rochette, *Peintres ant. ined.* 431 and supplement 452 is missing from the Stephani Catalogue of Vases in Leningrad. Where is it now? See also Eitrem, *op. cit.* 2488 ff.

[27] *Odyssey* 7, 197 ff.

[28] Museo Capitolino II a. Literature Stuart Jones, *Catalogue* 92.

[29] *De Dea Syria* 31 ff. Cf. Cumont, *RE* 4, 2243.

[30] Since the early Hellenistic temple of the time of Stratonike is described, the monument is probably contemporary. For the general motive, espe-

recognizably. More important, however, are the attributes, because they serve to trace the nature of the image as composed theologically of various single parts, for the analysis of which Lucian's account may be used. He describes a Panthea whose basic nature as Hera is probably expressed by the fact that she was the partner of a Zeus.[31] The traits of other goddesses which could also be seen in her must have been recognizable through the rest of her attributes because "on close scrutiny her appearance was manifold." Both Lucian and the Capitoline altar furnish her with lions, which assimilate her to Cybele. She has something of Aphrodite visible too: not merely the name which is often attributed to her[32] but the kestos which makes her a Uranic figure. The towerlike crown surrounded by rays mentioned by Lucian is replaced on the altar by a pointed cap shaped like the earlier papal tiaras, crowned by the crescent and with the veil of heaven flowing down. The Roman stone carver has awkwardly truncated the veil with the molding that passes underneath. In an association confirmed by Lucian, the entire headdress recalls Selene and Artemis, especially the Ephesian Artemis who wears a similar veil of heaven;[33] it is the adornment of a celestial goddess. But nothing in Lucian helps to explain the flat, round object with a handle held by the figure on the Acilius altar in her left hand, as the Hierapolis statue probably held a sceptre. What is meant, however, is undoubtedly a round mirror, another of Aphrodite's attributes; the Paredros of the Aventine Dolichenus[34] holds it in a very similar way. The awkward rendering, in the shape of a kitchen spoon, is likewise comparable. Something similar holds true for the object, up to now unexplained, in the right hand. It is definitely not a pomegranate[35] or any other fruit, though its centre, unlike the flat mirror, obviously suggests a three-dimensional, rounded form.

cially the arrangement of the animals of the figure from *Baalbeck, Ergebnisse der Ausgrabungen*, edited by Th. Wiegand 1, pl. 13 and 2, 122 ff.; it is a question of a goddess also related through the history of religion.

[31] Cumont, *loc. cit.* Wissowa, *Religion und Kultus*[2] 360 f.

[32] Wissowa, *op. cit.* 361. Most of the Lucian quotations occur also on inscriptions.

[33] H. Thiersch, "Artemis Ephesia," *AbhGöttingen* 12 (1935).

[34] Votive relief, Antiquario Comunale, *AA* (1935) 549 ff. Cf. Cumont, *op. cit.*, 2243.

[35] Suggested by Stuart Jones, *op. cit.*

It too is attached to a handle clasped rather awkwardly by the four fingers and the upturned thumb of the right hand. On first impression it seems larger than it actually is. Above the globular centre it terminates in a small round knob. The object can hardly be anything other than a spindle, which we would expect here anyway, since it was the only characteristic attribute of the statue at Hierapolis missing here and the only one which reminded Lucian of the Moirai. This now completes the image and puts it in full possession of its hieratic powers. The object might more precisely be called a distaff than a spindle; when the loose flax is wound around it, ready for spinning, it has the appearance of a round clew, as is attested by numerous vase paintings.[36] This form, which was, after all, rather uncommon (even if we take into consideration poor transmission and misunderstandings), may be compared with representations on Imperial coins of the Athena of Ilium, who also was provided with a spindle. On the coins of Julia Domna[37] one sees clearly that the implement can consist of two clews,[38] placed one on top of the other. Presumably we must look here for the origins of the strange knob on the Acilius altar. Actually the spinner while at work is busy with two such clews, one of flax on the distaff and another on the spindle which slowly takes up the thread. Blinkenberg established[39] that the Athena of Erythrae, said by Pausanias[40] to have held a spindle in each hand, actually held a distaff in one hand and a spindle in the other. The coins of Ilium probably show the same thing, only the two clews are fastened together like knitting equipment that has just been used and is now put aside. Thus, the slanting stick on Dörpfeld's item No. 93, actually thrust like a knitting needle through the lower clew, ought to be interpreted as a spool. Finally, this also helps to explain the strange representation of three spindles on another remarkable

---

[36] Cf. below, p. 63 n. 57.

[37] W. Dörpfeld, *Troja und Ilion* 2, Beilage 65, no. 92/93.

[38] Not required; the spindle can also be simple, cf. Dörpfeld, *op. cit.* supplement 61, nos. 16, 18/19.

[39] "L'Image d'Athana Lindia," *MeddelKopenhagen* 1, 2 (1917) 19 f., no. 4. The figure must have resembled the spinner on the beautiful silver ring in the British Museum, no. 1036, Catal. Marshall pl. 27.

[40] VII, 5, 9.

monument, a clay disc in the museum at Brindisi (Pl. XIX)[41] discussed by K. Kerényi. It must be like the one that served as a model
for the unusual shape of the spinning implement on the Acilius altar.
Furthermore, it leads us back, geographically and historically, to a
realm closely related to the Athena of Ilium: the spindle goddess is
at home in Asia Minor. The Syrian goddess on the Roman monument can furthermore be compared with a coin from Hierapolis,[42]
the details of which correspond more closely to Lucian's description.
Very likely it represents the cult image, and on the whole, it corroborates the connection between all these monuments most convincingly. It renders the authentic attributes of the towerlike crown
and sceptre, rather than the pointed cap and the otherwise unparalleled mirror.[43]

The cult at Hierapolis was not organized before Hellenistic times,
but the goddess, known as Atargatis or by some other name, definitely originates earlier.[44] Conceptually she incorporates various
elements, including the ancient image of the spinning goddess. At
an early stage she was associated with the great mother sanctuaries
of Asia Minor. These have been successfully traced with the exception of the reliefs from Nimrud; we do not have to repeat the
list of monuments here.[45] They are grouped around Picard's "dame
au fuseau",[46] the curious ivory statuette from the Ephesian Artemision, to which P. M. Schuhl has referred as earlier Oriental evi-

---

[41] *ARW* 30 (1933) 287 ff. Corresponding objects on disks from Taranto
prove that they are spinning tools; cf. A. J. Evans, *JHS* 7 (1886) 45, and
M. Daniel, *AJA* 28 (1924) 26 and 28. The epigram Kaibel 222, 7, *RE* 15,
2477 also implies a spindle for each Moira: "The compelling spindles of the
tireless Moirai." Thus, Kerényi's interpretation is confirmed, but the Platonic
whorls must be left out. The concept of destiny ruling the heavens is indeed
related.

[42] Bronze of Marcus Aurelius, cf. J. P. Six, *Num. Chronicle* 18 (1878) 119.
Fig. 42 in J. Garstang, *The Hittite Empire* 304, is probably a drawing of this
coin.

[43] The outstanding Hera from Ankyra, Imhoof-Blumer, *Kleinasiatische
Münzen* 1, pl. 7, 2 apparently also holds spindle and sceptre. She belongs in
the same category. For form of double clew cf. the spindle of Taras on coins
of the fifth century B.C., e.g. *Katalog Hirsch* 15 (1906) pl. 2, no. 385.

[44] Garstang, *op. cit.* 305 f. Cumont, *loc. cit.*

[45] Nimrud Reliefs, P. M. Schuhl, *RA* 32 (1930) 61 ff. and pl. 7. Von Salis,
Theseus und Ariadne 35.

[46] *Ephèse et Claros* 496 f., with literature.

dence for the goddess with the spindle in the Er myth, probably
with good reason.[47] We cannot analyze the nature of these related
though widely separated materials here. Relations between Dea
Syria and the Ephesian goddess exist also elsewhere and were, as
Lucian's account shows, already recognized in antiquity. That the
spindle belonged among the common maternal-feminine attributes
is proved for the Ephesian Artemis not only by the figurine of a
spinner found in her votive treasury but even more by the cogno-
men χρυσηλάκατος,[48] which makes her the mistress of the golden
spindle. Some Hittite reliefs from Marasch expressing the same
religious idea should probably be included in this broader context.
Here again we find the seated mother[49] or matron with kalathos,
mirror and spindle[50] (Pl. XX). The basic idea, expressed by venerable attributes, is generally the same. Even theological speculation,
unfortunately understandable only at a later stage, has preserved
a notion of the homogeneity of these beings and by preference made
them the object of mystic contemplation. Much is to be learned
from this for the conflation of goddess of fate, cosmic mother and
heavenly queen in the image of the Syrian goddess and similar
figures.[51] Only thereby is the totality of those global and governing
qualities rendered in a divine spinner; these qualities are the
essence of the Platonic Ananke and can only be realized by a universal goddess. Here she is enthroned as cult image in full view, a
celestial goddess, a spindle in her hand, endowed with almost un-
limited power over all things living and dead; here she proves to be
a genuine and ancient image of the myth. As far as she is called
Aphrodite—one of her many names—she is Urania,[52] and as such
she can eventually be found again in the Greek domain of Orphic
hymns. As celestial Aphrodite she is the mother of Ananke and

---

[47] Schuhl, *op. cit.*, 58 ff.

[48] F. Poulsen, *Delphische Studien* 10. Spindle in the Delphic cult of
Artemis, Schuhl, *op. cit.* p. 62.

[49] Garstang, *op. cit.* 230.

[50] Garstang, *op. cit.* 224; cf. Haas, *Bilderatlas z. Religionsgeschichte* 5,
Religion d. Hethiter, no. 14. Messerschmidt, *Corpus inscript. Hett.* 1, 18, pl. 22.

[51] Cumont, *op. cit.*, 2239 ff. Movers, *Phoenizier* 1, 598 ff. For the omni-
potence of celestial goddesses also M. P. Nilsson, *Gnomon* 12 (1936) 45.

[52] Evidence of the usual equation: Cumont, *op. cit.* 2240.

mistress of the three Moirai,[53] elsewhere the eldest of the Moirai.[54] Since Plato himself did not use the name Aphrodite in connection with Ananke, we do not have to enter into the Greek domain for the time being. But it does serve to reveal how this image of the spindle goddess could become a part of the existing concepts of the powers of fate in the story of Er, that is, simply by representing the Celestial being. A. Dieterich recognized in her the primal mother or rather one of the primal mothers of the Platonic Ananke.[55]

Thus, the account of the apparently dead, later resurrected man was an oriental fairy tale which Plato explicitly introduced through the narrator, and it is not surprising to come across, in the course of it, traces of a celestial or mother religion from Asia Minor; this is but one more proof of the validity of Plato's statement about its place of origin which was in any case beyond doubt.[56] If, however, the basic mythical concept from which the vision of Ananke evolved could be found there and named, then, going back to the text proper, it is almost possible now to set the dream image visibly side by side with its counterpart in mythical reality. That is, the dream image reveals its peculiar nature to the extent that it resembles its origin; however, it constantly incorporates it and changes it in the course of its own flowing transformations. As soon as one calls to mind the serene, mythical image on its throne, it expands beyond any imagery or mere description into more versatile spiritual purposes of its own and into a new world of ideas, where the myth can be told and at the same time interpreted. This lofty world of meanings is now astoundingly visible: there, figuration and interpretation become more intimately united at every turn; the simple comparison accomplished by the first words must be called its beginning; the spindle of the cosmic goddess is equal to the universe itself.

---

[53] *Orph. Hymns* 55, esp. v. 1/10.

[54] Inscription on the pillar of Aphrodite's sanctuary ἐν κήποις at Athens, *Paus.* I, 19, I.

[55] *Abraxas*, 101 f. Preliminary steps of a similar mythicizing of Ananke with the aid of Aphrodite theology also appear in philosophical literature, esp. Parmenides, fragm. 8, 37; cf. Gundel, *op. cit.* 13.

[56] Eisler, *Weltenmantel und Himmelszelt* 1, 97 f. In Arabic the sun is a spindle, Vollers, *ARW* 9 (1906) 179. Cumont, *Textes et Monuments* 1, 39. Also Schuhl, op. cit.

It is by now clear that the entire figure of the spinner we have just described is a necessary, though almost not explicit, prerequisite for this comparison. However, the comparison becomes the object of reflection, and in it here we must search for the hidden cause of the ensuing transformations up to the break between the interwoven images mentioned above. The comparison itself immediately implies a change in the transmitted image of the spinning mistress of the universe which indeed is established through the break. For where is the spindle in any of the images? We may recall that at the beginning of the passage 616 C the concept is literally intertwined with the spherical form of the universe that had been observed just previously. If one turns now to the monuments, not only the goddesses discussed above but other monuments in which women appear with the hand spindle, one notices that they almost always have a round and, depending on its meaning, spherical object. Though it is a part of the spinning gear, this is definitely not the spindle described by Plato in his story, but the distaff with the wool wound round it. Thus the Dea Syria of the Acilius altar holds it too. It is always represented as a large, round clew, which indeed it is at the moment the work begins, while the spindle, hanging down at the same time with the ends of the clewed-up thread, merely looks like a stick with a whorl or like a longish, spindle-like tool; thus, it really does not inspire comparison with the round cosmos.[57] On these monuments the celestial sphere nowhere resembles the spindle but rather the distaff, since it occasionally even displays crossed bands which obviously served to hold the clew of loose wool together.[58] One would think that the analogy with the celestial globe would be perfect. If instead Plato transferred the mythical comparison to the spindle, whose corresponding appearance in art is hardly demonstrable, there must be a reason,

---

[57] Besides the above-mentioned examples of spinning women, cf. tomb relief Mynno, Berlin, *Katal.* Blümel 3, pl. 33, with an especially clear picture of the spindle. Examples on red-figured vases Blümner, *Technologie* I, 132, figs. 48, 51; the entwined distaff may be confused with a mirror unless thread and spindle are visible. Distaff and spindle on Hellenistic tombstones of Cyrenaica, *AJA* 17 (1913) 162. Thanks go to L. Curtius for the reference.

[58] Spindle thrown down by recognized Achilles on mosaic from Sainte Colombe; *Inventaire d. Mosaïques de la Gaule* I, 198.

and that is: when they are in use, the distaff is motionless, whereas
the spindle turns. That, however, is the point of the myth; the
concept is to proceed from the visual impression of the world as
sphere to an understanding of the revolving spheres. Therefore not
even the image of the turning spindle is sufficient, for when the
distaff is empty, owing to the fully wound clew, the spindle ap-
proaches a spherical shape.[59] The spindle passes through the centre,
a miniature counterpart of the axis of the universe; again at the
top we find the hook made of adamant which distinguishes the
image of the spindle. In Pythagorean speculations about the appearance of the world there may even have been an analogy for it.[60]
Thus, the well-known picture of the spinner would only have had
to be slightly reinterpreted in order to correspond outwardly with
the theoretical picture of the universe. But if we read a little further,
we see that this would not do, either. Presently the eye gazes down-
ward and beholds the arrangement of the eight spheres in their
different latitudes, colours, revolutions and velocities[61] through
the airy, transparent shell, no longer in their outward appearance
but rather in a section through the centre of the universal sphere.
Eventually the idea of the web or clew is abandoned altogether in
order to describe the spheres vividly, and the whorl swings alone
around the axis of the spindle, that is, the structure of eight whorls
fitting into one another like bowls, the different sized rims of which,
open at the top, lie in the same plane. Thus, the miraculous working
of the spheres and their swinging harmony can be represented from
above (fig. 1). Only the logic of its laws produces this strange variation of the spinner's image, which was probably not shown like this
elsewhere.

Whether a whorl of similar construction ever served to make real

---

[59] Hence its Latin name *globus*, Blümner, *op. cit.*, 130. Spherical clews of
wool held by a seated woman on white-ground pyxis in the British Museum,
Catal. Vases 3, D 12, pl. 12. Cf. von Salis, *Theseus und Ariadne* 4.

[60] I.e. transmission by Stobaeus, *Ecl.* 1, 256, according to which the Pythagoreans assumed the cosmic sphere to have a conical peak of fire; cited by
Zeller, *op. cit.* 543, note, in a similar interpretation.

[61] For the transparency, cf. the model of the cosmos handed down by Hero
of Alexandria, *op. ed.* W. Schmidt (1889) L, 222 ff. no. 7 and fig. 51. Eisler
op. cit. I, 99. Occasionally the *sphaera* of Archimedes is mentioned as being
made of glass. Cf. Schlachter, *op. cit.* 51.

yarn is doubtful. The "scheme" of the whorl, its outward shape, does indeed resemble the everyday implement, as is explicitly stated, 616 D. Whorls are by nature round objects; their basic form varies from a disc to a globe;[62] consequently this one is shown as a hemisphere in section seen from above. Its inner arrangement of seven hemispheres inside the outermost one is all the more unusual. No hitherto discovered real whorl is like it, and the one in the Mainz

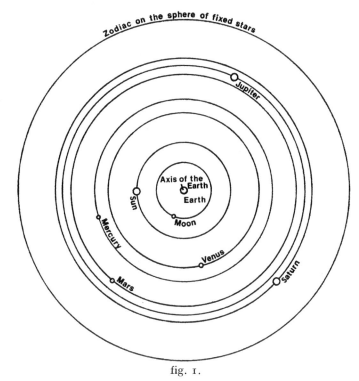

fig. 1.

Museum, mentioned occasionally, only seemingly[63] resembles it. Schuhl has already shown that an example from Ephesus corresponds more closely with Plato's "view from above".[64] This object does have concentric circles decorating the surface, but of course it is all one piece. A disc-like whorl made of bone, in the British Museum,

---

[62] Ebert, *Reallexikon f. Vorgeschichte* 13, 268 (Textiltechnik).
[63] According to Blümner, *op. cit.* 125, fig. 46.
[64] *RA* 32 (1930) 62 and pl. 6.

may prove that the ornamentation with concentric circles continues over a long period (Pl. XXI).[65] How remarkably well such top-like implements can serve as images of the celestial sphere is shown by comparing them with one of the schematic diagrams of the sky which, to illustrate the structure of the universe, remained in use up to the late Middle Ages (fig. 2).[66] The Platonic metaphor of hemi-spherical bowls fitting into one another is confirmed by the disc-like surface produced but the rest of the arrangement presented as real is not. This is Plato's unique invention, and it served solely as

fig. 2.

---

[65] Pl. XXI courtesy of R. Hinks, British Musem.

[66] Calendar picture from *El Acabóse del ano y nuevo* de 1934, 42. Probably from Cortès, *Lunario*; fig. 2 courtesy of the Warburg Library. Plato's perception of the eight spheres is of course schematic and pictorial, not real, cf. Adam, *op. cit.*, as it is in the somewhat different description in the Timaeus, 36 d; cf. A. E. Taylor, *Comment. of Timaeus* 147 and 150; perhaps a reminiscence of the original conception of rings instead of spheres into which the celestial bodies are fitted, thereby sharing their motion, Taylor, *loc. cit.* The sirens of the octave can sit on them. At that time all these concepts changed from conceptions of planes (circles) to those of volumes (spheres), cf. E. Pfeiffer, *op. cit.* 112 for meaning of the word ἄντυξ. Later Platonism characteristically applied without hesitation ἄτρακτος to the entire (spherical) heaven, e.g. Plotinus, *Enn.* 2, 3, 9; cf. Boeckh, *op. cit.* 312.

illustration of the theory of the sphere in its special form. It arises from the possibility of relating a real object, constructed like the mechanism of the cosmos, to the image of the mythical spinner, who is always known as a superordinate concept. For this the comparison with the flat whorl would no longer suffice; the same holds true for the potter's wheel which was earlier used with a similar intention.[67] The possible implementation of such an instrument should be considered cautiously because we know so little; several elaborately playful variations, unknown to us, may have existed for some needs or cults. A fine and noteworthy bronze in Naples (Pl. XXII),[68] shows a carefully worked structure of eight stacked whorls on a spindle; however, they are disc-like, not hemispherical. Two of them in the middle are connected perpendicularly by wires with rings attached on which small pieces of metal hung close together; when rotated, they touched each other, producing a tinkling, perhaps harmonized sound a, direct counterpart to the singing sirens of the octave of the spheres. Where the rims of the eight hemispheres are visible lying as concentric circles in a plane, there can no longer be any shafts like those discussed a short time ago. In this moment at least, the spherical appearance of the whole is apparently given up and actually two different pictures emerge which, though they are closely connected, are actually incompatible. According to the intention which is to be expressed, it is a matter of a sphere with the spindle attached to its ἄχρα, then of hemispheres, the whorls. The break discussed above, which corroborates the division undertaken by Adam,[69] is now completely clear. Both statements are allegorically valid for the universe; the two images are not parts of a systematic deduction but of a slowly developing, dream-like, optical and mythical vision. Therein lies their inner unity. Properly speaking, each of them, but especially the image of the whorl, is a didactic metaphor created by deliberately interpreting a cosmography together with mythical, basic ideas; it is a mythico-poetic allegorical interpretation.

---

[67] Schuhl, *RA* 31 (1930), 249.

[68] Maiuri, *BPI* 40 (1914) 175 ff. Similar pieces in the *Brit. Mus.* cabinet G 413.

[69] *Op. cit.*; cf. above p. 52 n. 5.

In the following passage, the three Moirai come into view of the souls, that is of the reader: clad in white vestments and with filleted heads, they sit round, each one on her throne. The mythical space becomes clearer and more animated but at the same time, the concept of the universe loses its earlier solitude and exclusiveness. The new change of dimensions is carried out here (617 C), and the world spindle or globe, or both in one, floats while oscillating in the middle between the four celestial beings who help to turn it, now touching the outer limits, now the inner mechanism. Thereby a third transformation of the general idea has been added, no less dream-like than the previous one but gradually shifting the idea to a completely new setting. Soon the until now enormous creatures begin to associate actively with the wanderers; then a herald appears whose opening words are very like an official proclamation;[70] and a half solemn-judicial, half gloomy-underworld ceremony becomes more and more recognizable through an increasing number of well-known allusions. Ananke, the celestial goddess and immaterial[71] law of the world who is freed from being an abstraction to incarnate in a form that fused together various related memories, is transferred as supreme mistress into this mythical realm in order to connect celestial and underworld, universal law and human fate. Thus the last and most personal form of her mythicizing is achieved. She corresponds almost as a kind of Persephone, to Orphic and Pythagorean beliefs, where she finally found her permanent place in Greek myth as Erinys, Adrasteia, or the ruling mistress of the dead.[72] If any pictorial representations of her existed at all, they seem to have belonged in this circle and correspond to these ideas.[73]

---

[70] A strange passage already noticed by Proclus; cf. Adam, *op. cit.* 454, commentary.

[71] Damascios 123 bis; Diels, *Vorsokratiker* I, 12 (Orpheus).

[72] Description of the Orphic Ananke esp. in A. Dieterich, *Nekyia* 122 ff. Maass, *Orpheus* 268 ff.; equation with Persephone 273 n.57. Gundel, *op. cit.* 21 ff. and 27 ff.

[73] Representation on vase Benndorf, *Griech. und sizil. Vasenbilder*, pl. 36, 9 must be called apocryphal on account of the uncertain reading. A more likely reading is that of the inscription NAN above an Erinys-like figure on underworld krater from Altamura, Naples 3222 as Ananke because the concept of Furies in the realm of the underworld is otherwise documented,

As far as they were able to enter into the concepts and imagination of such daemons and goddesses of the dead, they fall outside the scope of this investigation; the problem of Ananke's relation to the spherical image of the cosmos is for our purposes solved.

cf. Maass, *op. cit.* W. *Vorlegeblätter*, Serie E, pl. 2, ought to be looked at more closely. Winkler, "Darstellung der Unterwelt" 131, *Breslauer Abh.* 5 (1868) 25.

CHAPTER FIVE

THE CELESTIAL SPHERE OF THE MOIRAI

Several representations of the Moirai belong in the same category of mythical-allegorical meaning; they continue it directly, like variations on a theme.

We begin with the strange relief in the Dresnay collection (Pl. XXIII). The piece passed through many hands before it came to its present owner. In the auction catalogue of the collection of J. Ferroni[1] it is said to have come from the Museo Nani, a piece of information not repeated in the two publications by Biagi.[2] Considering its state of preservation and as far as can be ascertained from the photograph, it is likely that it is an old museum piece. I am indebted to F. Cumont for the reference as to its present whereabouts together with the following text from the unavailable catalogue of the collection P. Perdrizet.[3]

"Relief des Parques—Marbre blanc. Hauteur 63 cm. Longueur 1,33 m. Ce marbre a fait partie de la collection Nani. Il a été acheté à Rome en 1912.

Restauration: bras et épaule du putto gauche.

Long côté d'un sarcophage, destiné d'après le sujet à un adolescent. A gauche un amour ailé, qui apprend le ceste sous la direction d'un paidotribe de son âge, vêtu du manteau et tenant la baguette des instructeurs.

A droite, trois fillettes du même âge, que les deux petits personnages de gauche, sont représentées en Parques. Celle de droite

---

[1] *Catalogue de la Vente Gioacchino Ferroni*, (Rome, 1909) no. 277, 33, and pl. 52. I owe the information about this collection to the kindness of G. Sangiorgi.

[2] Cl. Biagi, *Monumenta ex Museo J. Nanii Veneti* (Rome, 1785 and 1787).

[3] Transcription and information about text of catalogue in a letter from F. Cumont of Feb. 19, 1933: P. Perdrizet, *Antiquités Grecques de la collection du Vicomte du Dresnay*, Chateau du Dréneuc (Loire inférieure), 1918. Parcae relief pl. 19. Cf. *Rev. études grecques* 33 (1920) 96 (Pottier).

lit un volumen à demi déroulé, celle du milieu file, celle de gauche
cherche sur un globe l'heure ou l'horoscope.

Sur le sarcophage du Louvre (Clarac 216, Nr. 768; Fröhner,
Sculpt. d. L. Nr. 490) l'une des Parques indique sur une sphère
la γένεσις du défunt.

Époque impériale."

This description hardly needs to be expanded. The Nani Museum
owned many pieces found in Greece and this relief has many details
which belie Greek workmanship of the Roman period. A survival
of late Hellenistic traditions within the generally classicistic style
is still recognizable in the loose arrangement of figures as in the
rather fine drapery motives. Although this piece cannot be judged
without further research we may question whether its identification
as the long side of a sarcophagus will withstand scrutiny. Even if
it is a Greek work it is unlikely to be such, and among Roman
sarcophagi, it must also be considered quite an isolated case.[4]
Furthermore, the present state of the relief ie definitely incomplete
because the boxer on the left side must have had at least one op-
ponent, in which case it remains uncertain whether still more
scenes followed. Since the long side of a sarcophagus cannot be put
together from several plates, the end of this piece must have been
finished in modern times. The representation itself seems to have
been reworked in some places, for example the face and the raised
distaff of the spinner. In any case we must assume a funerary meaning for the figural motives, not only for the group of the Parcae
but also for the boxing Erotes. Indeed, similar motives become
quite common later, on Roman sarcophagi.[5] The faces of the seated
Parca and also the reading one serve best to indicate a date; their
Livia-like coiffures, which appear already in the late Hellenistic

---

[4] G. Rodenwaldt kindly confirmed this statement. He considered a parallel to be the sarcophagus in the Louvre, AZ 43 (1885) 209 ff. and pl. 14,
comparable in its rather loose composition; the date of the relief is mid
second century A.D., confirming the connection with the contemporary art
of sarcophagi.

[5] Cf. Relief Colonna, EA 1166; playing Erotes with mask, Geneva, EA
(1896). Palaestra scenes as a standing motive on sarcophagi with Erotes are
well known.

period, are early Claudian. Thus the whole must have been a continuous frieze, not a sarcophagus; perhaps it belonged to a small sepulchral building, the complete extent of which can no longer be determined.

The Parcae, the only group that has any meaning for our considerations, have no discernible relation to the athletic representation next to them. It is a peculiarly separate composition which seems to have proportions different from its companions. It is not even certain that those who are represented are really meant to be children of the same age or playing Erotes, because only their relatively small size distinguishes them. Their activity is not one of the usual travesties which children, Erotes, and Psychai normally perform on similar occasions in funerary art. Moreover, the meaning of the travesty would be hard to interpret in this case.

The Parcae's occupation, on the other hand, is obvious even if strange. The general idea of destiny that underlies their occupation is broken up into the division of labor popular from early Roman times. Its earliest example, neo-Attic rather than classical, is the group of Moirai on the Madrid puteal, and its replicas.[6] The spinner, logically to be regarded as Clotho, enacts their former common activity there, as here, alone. On the Dresnay relief she is further defined and now probably also suggests the metaphor of death, through the snapping of the spun thread so often found in literature.[7] Her sister on the right who reads from a scroll is probably the successor of Atropos on the puteal, the scroll replacing what was originally a writing-tablet; both concepts, writing as well as reading, belong to her and were absorbed in the gradually conventionalized literary and artistic types of the three Parcae, reading perhaps also

---

[6] P. Arndt, *EA* 1724/29. W. Amelung, *EA* 2990. The style and costume of the Moirai remain incompatible with the art of the Parthenon, in spite of R. Carpenter's energetic attempts, *Hesperia* 2 (1933) 42 ff.; also with Agorakritos, cf. *ibid.*, 63. For reconstruction of Lachesis, *ibid.*, 56 ff., see M. Wegner, *AM* 57 (1932) 92 ff. and L. Curtius, *Die antike Kunst* 2, 223. R. Schneider, *Geburt der Athene* 35 correctly noted that the conception of the triple activity of the Moirai which is fully developed on the puteal cannot belong to the fifth century B.C.

[7] E. Steinbach, *Der Faden der Schicksalsgottheiten* 37 ff.

because it was already characteristic for an early Italic Parca.[8]
The figurative representation offers here as often elsewhere the op-
portunity to unite in one symbol two originally different ideas,
for both of which there are plenty of examples. While the Moira
with the writing-tablet on the Madrid puteal is distinguished from
Lachesis by the lots, later on the latter will frequently, especially
on sarcophagi, take the place of the reading Parca,[9] as she probably does on the Dresnay relief where the Moira with the lots is left
out. The Parca who sits opposite must be Atropos; her attention
is turned to the large sphere on the ground between the three of
them, which seems to be their common attribute. This sphere is
the most unusual and thereby the most interesting element of the
whole monument. It is set upon the same small base which was
mentioned above several times in connection with Urania or with
scholars. Considering the way in which the seated figure points at it
with her radius,[10] one might identify her as the Muse Urania whose
image here stands in for Moira. The problem lies in the fact that
such a switch could actually take place between the originally
quite separate artistic concepts of the celestial Muse with the sphere,
and the Moirai. The allocation of the sphere to the Moirai or to one
Moira, which has such a transparent meaning in the case of Urania,
can no longer be explained as a simple metaphor like the snapping
of the thread on the reading of the book of fate.[11] There the metaphors arise as a very pointed application of old magical-religious
symbols originating in the mythical past of the Fates. The sphere,
however, wherever it was connected in art with the Moirai, was not
one of those symbols. It belongs even less than the spindle or book

---

[8] For reading and writing Fate among Etruscans and Romans, F. Messerschmidt, *ARW* 29 (1931) 60 ff. The concept of reading among the Greeks,
Eitrem, *RE* 15, 2485; Steinbach, *op. cit.* 19.

[9] Messerschmidt, *op. cit.* 68. She figured as Clotho on the fragment of the
sarcophagus in the Vatican, *Katal.* Amelung 2, 541, no. 353, here Pl. XXVI
where the relation to the names has disappeared.

[10] See above, p. 11. She holds the corner of the cloak in her left hand
like Nemesis, cf. L. Curtius, *Festschrfit James Loeb* 60.

[11] Cf. the famous verse Martial 10, 44, 6: Gaudia tu differs, at non et
stamina differt Atropos, atque omnis scribitur hora tibi, a strange version
of the idea of Carpe diem, *RömMitt.* 49 (1934) 158 f. Eitrem, *op. cit.* 2484.
On reading for the determination of death, Messerschmidt, *op. cit.* 68.

with the old mythical concept of the virtually inactive Moira mentioned above. Instead, what we are dealing with is the inclusion of the
new, expanded concept of fate, inherently abstract and speculative,
within the area of pictorial expression. This results in an image
like the one in Plato's vision where the three Moirai are gathered
around the globular cosmos, the immanent law of which they ad-
minister. Ananke is absent from this circle as a visible figure because in the capacity of all-encompassing Necessity, she was absorbed in this idea of fate which, by now a symbolic image of the
universe, has joined the mythical image of the Moirai. From now on
the attributive trio of the Parcae with the celestial sphere replaces it.
Nevertheless it is strange that this leads to a new religious and
abstract development in art only, based on already available pictorial concepts. The sphere as an attribute for a Moira is no longer
attested in literature. In the new pictorial constellation, which it
entered as an eloquent expression of changing combinations of
thought, it gains an independent allegorical life within the myth.

Since the Dresnay relief offers only casually ascertainable evidence, the beginning remains uncertain: for the time being, it is not
possible to say when the Parcae were furnished with the celestial
sphere. Still, there is a strange observation in Pausanias[12] which,
considering its wording, we must examine in the search for older prototypes. It comes in the description of the chryselephantine table in
the inventory of the Heraion at Olympia that served for the exhibi-
tion of victory wreaths. Its maker was one Colotes of uncertain
origin, born probably in one of the cities called Heraclea.[13] On the
four sides of the table were reliefs mostly with single gods set side
by side, so that a connective action is not recognizable in Pausanias'
description. He reports the following gathering on one end of the
table: Pluto, carrying the key to Hades, Dionysos, Persephone,
and nymphs, one of whom held a sphere.

Pausanias did not indicate—he probably did not know—what
kind of sphere it was, and his identification of the female beings

---

[12] Pausanias V, 20, 1. I wish to thank E. Kraiker for reminding me of
this passage.
[13] For Colotes, G. Lippold, *RE* 1120; M. Bieber, *Thieme-Becker, Künst-
lerlexikon*, s.v.; L. Curtius, *Die antike Kunst* 2, 267.

with the sphere as nymphs is not entirely certain. But it is obvious
that the group of gods joined by these nymphs was not accidental
without reason. It included Pluto and Persephone, the reigning
couple of the underworld; next to them Pausanias recognized
Dionysos, not a familiar sight in the subterranean realm; his attributes probably identified him. This mention may be added to the
limited number of testimonies which disclose relations between
Dionysos and the underworld.[14] This observation leads to yet another: the triad of Pluto and Persephone with Dionysos standing
before them, or Dionysos alone before Persephone, is documented on
Locrian reliefs which predate the hypothetical activity of Colotes
by a little less than one generation.[15] As we have already read in
Pausanias' description, in mute confrontation the gods sit or stand
here. Also present in this circle are those female beings who approach the mistress of the underworld bearing a globular object;[16]
Pausanias, if he had a similar representation in mind, might easily
have called them nymphs carrying a sphere. The peculiar gathering
of gods he describes on this side of the table[17] could not be better
illustrated. Only the identification of the sphere-bearers is still not
satisfactory. We must consider five main types:

1. Orsi *BdA* 3 (1909), 413, fig. 6; same Quagliati *Ausonia* 3 (1908),
   fig. 47. L. Curtius, *Die antike Kunst* 2, 212.

---

[14] W. F. Otto, *Dionysos* 106 ff., esp. 108 f., Heraclitus' equation between
Dionysos and Hades.

[15] P. Orsi, *BdA* 3 (1909) 414, fig. 7; 416, fig. 9, description on 424. Photographs of the same types Q. Quagliati, *Ausonia* 3 (1908) 175 ff. Cf. Oldfather,
Philologus 69 (1910) 115.

[16] P. Orsi, *op. cit.*, 412 ff; Q. Quagliati, *Ausonia, op. cit.* 197 ff.

[17] In order to have reliefs on all four sides, the table must have resembled
the box-like furnishings on the Locri plaques, e.g. *Ausonia* 3 (1908) 195, ← pl.
fig. 47. Perhaps Colotes with his eccentric ideas—he put the rooster of the
goddess of the earth and the underworld on top of the helmet of an Athena—
came from a place that had just such an ancient earth and underworld cult
as required the votives related to his objects; i.e. the Sicilian instead of the
Elic Herakleia if the Lucanian was really not founded earlier than the
traditional date of 432 B.C. Cf. *RE* 8, 423, no. 28 and 30. For the rooster of
the Elic Athena, recall the heraldic animal of the Panathenaea. Pausanias
offered other explanations besides the probably incorrect attribution to
Phidias, VI, 26, 3. Cf. Lippold *op. cit.*

2. Orsi fig. 5, description of both 423 f.
3. Quagliati 199, fig. 48.
4. Quagliati 224, fig. 73.
5. The complete plate, the uppermost fragment of which was listed by Orsi 420, now published by Zancani Montuoro, in the memorial volume for P. Orsi, *Archivio Storico per la Calabria e la Lucania*, 1935, 195 ff. (Pl. XXIV).

The scheme is virtually the same in each case: that of the offering of votives. Standing before the enthroned Persephone is the offering bearer with the globular object in one hand on 1, 2 and 5, and the indispensable rooster in the other. On 3 and 4 the other hand holds a bulging fold of the garment which is formed by the overfall of the peplos; on 4 it seems to contain fruit; 3 is not quite clear but it is probably empty. The sphere on 1 does not have any distinguishing mark; on 2 it is encircled by crossed bands; on 3 it seems to have a rhomboid design and a figured band that is wound around the middle; on 4 it is not clearly visible. Two variants[18] exist of 5, of like shape but differently worked; one similar to 3 only without band and with tiny narrow squares, the other closely covered with dots, as they appeared on other reliefs of this category to identify garments or materials perhaps made of wool.[19] The pose of the small figure on 5, certainly a female, is peculiar; instead of holding her sphere in the palm of her hand, she lets it float under her downturned palm, possibly hanging from a string or loop[20] added in paint. Behind her stands the much larger, bearded Ares whom P. Zancani Montuoro has already described; strangely he brings the enthroned goddess her rooster just a it is presented elsewhere by the votary together with the globe. In this gathering of gods the small

---

[18] Zancani Montuoro, *op. cit.* 208.

[19] E.g. Peplas and Kolpos of the fruit-gatherer, Quagliati, *op. cit.* 223, fig. 71.

[20] The conjecture of the editor that the sphaira is meant to be dropped into the goddess' phial goes against the manner of representation of the period; the delivery of an object would be differently depicted, as the bowl should be,—it is not meant to catch balls. Besides, the position of the offerer's fingers indicates an activity, i.e. holding something between thumb and forefinger.

figure cannot be an ordinary mortal woman. No clue is given, particularly since in this entire group of reliefs there are certainly no human sacrificial processions; on the other hand real gods, such as the above mentioned Dionysos, approach as worshipers the enthroned couple or goddess who are doubtlessly rulers in their own domain. When Hermes pulls his ram along as an offering, he has to submit to a diminution otherwise unknown to him[21] by comparison with the other, apparently "big" gods. Thus, there are in their realm serving gods,[22] and the female figure with the enigmatic sphere must be one of these; she, in front of Ares, pays her respects to the ruling mistress.[23] Moreover, she has sisters. Hence, the girls who again in another scene carry singlehanded[24] or in a group[25] the beautifully woven peplos of the goddess, proceeding[26] directly behind or even before her, cannot be mortal women either. They are divine but nameless servants and acolytes, and Pausanias' identification of similar figures in Colotes' gathering of the gods, as well as that of the other participants, can also be applied to the Locrian reliefs. They are indeed nymphs and belong in the great hall of the underworld as companions and playmates of Demeter and Persephone;[27] in accordance with their primary meaning they were perhaps weavers,[28] hence occupied above all with preparing the garment of the goddess. Her relationship to them is similar to that of Athena to the tutelaries of the arrhephorai, the nymph-like sisters Herse and Pandrosos who sit upon the chests and folded

---

[21] Orsi, *op. cit.* 416, fig. 10.

[22] Cf. Oldfather, *op. cit.* 116.

[23] Nothing points to a trial, Zancani Montuoro, *op. cit.* 214 ff. Apart from the difficulty of identifying the female figure as "soul" which would be unparalleled, South-Italian Orphic art had a definite type for the judges of the dead, which is definitely not represented here. Moreover no action is shown that might be expected at a "trial."

[24] Orsi, *op. cit.* 421, fig. 17.

[25] *Ibid.*, 426 f., figs. 25/26.

[26] The goddess has the cup in which the kykeon is prepared, and she holds a little stick for stirring. Cf. L. Curtius, *op. cit.* 2, 212.

[27] Porphyrios, *De antro Nympharum*, ch. 7. More evidence *ML* s.v. Nymphen 516.

[28] Cf. observations by Porphyrios, *op. cit.* ch. 3, concerning the furnishings of the Homeric cave of the nymphs with vessels and looms of stone on which purple fabrics are woven; the inventory of Circe's dwelling.

clothes in the east pediment of the Parthenon.[29] Now, if the goddess of the underworld is returned to her chair, as she is seen on the Pinax type 1, bowl in hand, the little stick leaning against the garment folded up in front of her like a bale of cloth, the girl with rooster and globular object standing facing her; or if this girl, as on the fragment of type 4, offers fruit with her left hand while the right holds the sphere, and on another fragment[30] one of her sisters gathers fruit from the tree of Hades, putting it carefully into the kolpos of her dress; then the common denominator of serving becomes evident for all these beings. They are the nymphs of the goddess of Hades, one of whom Pausanias saw depicted on Colotes' table with a sphere in her hand. He could not have chosen a more felicitous name for them.

Considering the sphere itself, Quagliati[31] and Curtius[32] have already explained that it is a ball, which is most likely if one starts with its nature, inferred from the various representations. We cannot undertake to review once again the many speculations of Orphic and so-called Pythagorean literature where Sphaira is discussed as a symbol open to any meaning.[33] The interpretation as cosmos and celestial image, not only throughout later antiquity but already in early Platonism and its forerunners, is perfectly reasonable in the connection which we have investigated here and will not surprise us further with any new evidence. It inevitably became the general view after art had also grasped the idea of the sphere as a hieroglyph for the entire universe, especially the heavens, and had begun to use it at will. Hence it is understandable that the same explanation was applied to the sphere which, as mythical symbol of various cults and within the so-called Orphic religion, was attested even by the title of a poem ascribed either to the cult's founder, or to Linus.[34] What is interesting here, with respect to a sanctuary of un-

---

[29] L. Curtius, op. cit. 222. Pandrosos, the first spinner, ML s.v. 1531. For relation of Arrhephoroi and Hersephorai, L. Deubner, Attische Feste 9 ff.

[30] Quagliati, op. cit. 223, fig. 71.

[31] Ibid., 200.

[32] Ibid., 212.

[33] Cf. Zancani Montuoro, op. cit. 215 f.

[34] Orphicorum Fragmenta, edited by O. Kern, 314, 27.

derworldly deities that is close to Orphism as far as authentic monuments go, is the question what real role the symbol originally possessed in the cult or in its myth. Even if the monuments confirm
the texts so far as to attest to the occurrence of the sphere among sacred objects at the sanctuary of Persephone at Locri already around
430 B.C., it is apparent that real customs and mythical concepts
later generated the cosmic speculations in the philosophy of
religion. Such a process of generation is perceptible here, and even
as a cult object handed to the servants of the underworld mistress
and offered to her as part of her mythical domestic goods like the
rooster and garment, wool-basket or mirror. First we must investi-
gate its real meaning, obviously only the foundation of the allegorical
one pieced together from other concepts. Fortunately, the ancient
tradition itself seems to provide the answer. Spheres were known to
the ancients as belonging among the sacred symbols of the mysteries
of Dionysos son of Zeus, and Persephone; these were regarded as
balls and included among the toys of the divine child who, lured by
them, fell into the hands of the Titans who dismembered him.
Therefore the balls were, according to a doctrine traceable to
Orpheus himself, part of such ritual symbols as dice, tops, apples,
mirrors and other things.[35] But the infant Zeus also played with such
a ball whose gold-and-sky-blue stripes could not have been made
more beautiful even by Hephaistos; and it seems in this tale that
not the child but his nurse was the original owner of the precious
toy: it was made by the nurse Adrasteia in the Idaean cave[36].
She is shown on coins with the child on her arm, the sphere a toy
at her feet.[37] The round objects held by nymphs on the Locrian
reliefs are rather close to this conception. Their appearance and
decorations hardly allow them to be interpreted as anything but
playthings; this explains the fanciful ornamentation of their surface, appropriate to balls made of many-coloured bits of cloth,

---

[35] Clement of Alexandria, *Protreptikos* 2, 17; Arnobius, *adv. nationes* 5,
19; both passages in Kern, *Orphic. Fragmenta* 110, 34.
[36] Apollonius Rhodius, *Argonautica* 3, 132 ff. The later interpretation
combined Adrasteia with Nemesis-Ananke, the conception thereby touching the domain of the underworld goddess, cf. above and *RE* 1, 406; Marshall
M. Gilles, *The Argonautica Book* 3, 18.
[37] Imhoof-Blumer, *JdI* 3 (1888) 290 and pl. 9, 19.

leather or network which are well enough known from children's games.[38] Their light weight allowed them to be carried on a string, as on type 5; this may be verified by other examples. On the vase in Naples which O. Jahn correctly explained,[39] one of Europa's playmates carries her ball on a loop while she extends her right hand to adorn Zeus, the bull, with a wreath. When we add to all of this the confirming evidence of the Orphic tradition, which referred to its own mythical spheres as toy balls, this interpretation is indeed highly likely. Moreover, a coherent review of the Locri plaques will certainly produce new material since the representations in many respects explain one another. We can ignore the still un-answered question whether the significance of the "Orphic" spheres as toys, which evidently applies to reliefs and provides a mythical explanation, was in fact their first meaning. For a very instructive example of later allegorical attempts, we refer to Johannes Lydus, who thought the spheres of the Dionysiac mysteries represented the earth, and the mirrors heaven.[40] His reference to Plato's statement about the globular shape of the earth is definitely an interpretation anachronistic for the Locrian reliefs; the well-known passage in the *Phaedo* seems to be one of the earliest testimonies that they were widely known.[41] Nevertheless there might be a kernel of truth in what Johannes Lydus considered to be a relation between the mythical spheres and the earth, that is, the recollection of their belonging to the myths of Hades whose nymphs carry them there, just as they did at the gathering of the gods of the underworld on Colotes' table. On the other hand, in such images concepts were

---

[38] Quagliati, *loc. cit.* I owe to L. Curtius the reference to the collection of material in Wolters, *MJb* 8 (1913) 86 ff. On the vessel from Taranto dis-cussed there, fig. 4, a boy plays with a ball with crossed bands like the one in our type 2. Such crossed bands appear very often, cf. Daremberg-Saglio, s.v. *Pila.*

[39] Jahn, *Entführung der Europa* 2 and pl. 1. Cf. *RömMitt* 45 (1930) 224, n. 1. Ball carried by Eros on loop on South-Italian rhyton, British Museum, here Pl. XXV from museum photograph.

[40] *De Mens* 4, 51, Wuensch ed. 108.

[41] Phaedo 108 c. Perhaps Timaeus 55 D was in the mind of Johannes Lydus. For scientific knowledge of the shape of the world among the Greeks, E. Frank, *Plato und die sogen. Pythagoreer* 184 ff.; cf. P. Friedländer, *Platon* 243.

formed that made it easier later to transfer the sphere to the Moirai[42] who, outgrowing their likewise underworldly, nymphlike origin, developed new characteristics. But the sphere was unknown in their mythology. Persephone's nymphs could even be perceived as dancing Moirai, just as the ὄλβιοι Μοῖραι lead the chorus of the netherworld in Aristophanes' *Frogs*.[43]

Thus we find a sphere in the hands of originally nameless beings, mythical sisters of the Moirai who occasionally even take their name. Yet the interpretation as image of the universe was at that time certainly not given to the ball that was a mythical or cult object. It was added only in the course of time as in the case of the already cited toy of the infant Zeus. It is not yet possible to observe the various phases of this presumed development and the changes of meaning related to it. The relief once in the Museo Nani shows that these had long since been accomplished when they were incorporated into art. On the other hand the motive, once accepted, deeply influenced the representation of the Moirai in Imperial times. It actually united their artistic formation with the increasing abstract concept of fate. This process ultimately led to a completely new, definitive definition of the three goddesses and their activity, now within the playful freedom of allegorical symbols. Art once more undertook to describe the entirety of the world in significant metaphors springing from the treasure of its old and immense cultural awareness.

Now our inquiry turns to already surveyed and partly tilled soil: the position of the Moirai in the Platonizing anthropological system intended to be illustrated by the Prometheus sarcophagi[44] is well known. From their earlier history the Moirai kept the spindle and book while the sticks for drawing lots seem to have disappeared for good. The sphere has become a conventional attribute, losing any trace of its mythical-symbolic character; it is to be interpreted as

---

[42] The Athenians considered the Aglaurids to be Moirai, Hesychius s.v. Ἀγλαυρίδες; *ML* s.v. *Pandrosos*. If so, the "Moirai" indeed belonged at the birth of Athena on the Parthenon pediment, of which the neo-Attic puteal is one of our few later reflections.

[43] *Frogs* 449 ff. *Orphic Hymns* 43, 7. Cf. B. B. Rogers, *Comedies of Aristophanes* 5, 69.

[44] C. Robert, *Die antiken Sarkophagreliefs* 3, 3, 436 ff. Cf. Eitrem, *RE* 15, 2490 ff.

the celestial globe, and sometimes possesses crossed bands. The complete equation of the carrier of the sphere with similar types of representation, such as the celestial Muse Urania, is a natural consequence of the art-historical development and is quickly accomplished.[45] The way is now clear to present any given personification, equipped with appropriate attributes, in an image of the same figure; Martianus Capella, for example, endowed his Geometry with the celestial appearance, having her hold the globe with one hand and point to it with the radius.[46] This is the beginning of those personifications that freeeze into a single action or movement which then became the patrimony of medieval and later art as functional allegories. These can be traced best in the conception of the Cardinal Virtues. But this is not the primary intention of the Prometheus sarcophagi; rather they are trying to present, in their better replicas, a rationally clear action. The fragment in the Vatican, Robert no. 354 (Pl. XXVI), is the most complete example for the Parcae, as it was correctly interpreted by Jahn and Robert. What is shown is the casting of the horoscope: Atropos, after reading the exact time from a sundial, turns to Lachesis in order to impart it to her. The latter can thereupon point with the radius to the constellation on her globe or, as on the Capitoline replica,[47] take note of it in ink. The spinner, now superfluous, is missing in this arrangement. The old meaning of the word is lost when her name Clotho is given to the sister with the book who might also have been abandoned if her task had not been to keep representing the old, weird reading daemon of death.[48] The ancient concept of the spinning sisters and subterranean sorceresses was so completely absorbed and digested by the new representational possibilities that hardly anything of it remained; instead the sundial replaced it as a new attribute serving to complete the investigation of the celestial sphere. Characteristically, even this can be made independent as demonstrated on one

---

[45] Moira with globe on the Paris examples, Robert, *op. cit.* 351 and 356, or Lachesis on the Vatican fragment Robert no. 354, here Pl. XXVI. Compare with it the usual Urania type, e.g. Vatican, Croce greca 580, or Munich, Glyptothek 326 (Pl. VIII). Bie, *Die Musen* 80 f.

[46] Above, p. 73.

[47] Robert *op. cit.* 442, no. 355.

[48] *Ibid.*, 443.

end of the sarcophagus in Naples;[49] without intimate knowledge of the context, nobody would recognize the female figure as a Moira who obviously hurries toward a sundial, presumably to determine the position of the stars at the moment of the birth of a new human being.

For this is the actual question. It is a case of an artful, comprehensive system of the world wherein the concept of fate, removed now permanently from mythical piety, has spiritually joined the laws of the universe, whose effectiveness is recognized in practice in the belief in astrology.[50] Into these laws of matter the reluctant Anima enters as soon as the human being is born and they form the destiny which is the subject of representations on sarcophagi. The causal connection of the basic human facts of birth and death is represented by the old, only seemingly mythical images as the actual essence of religious experience and scientific cognition,[51] which we cannot examine more closely here. This common fate is determined for the individual by the configuration of the planets; the Moirai are no longer fate's rulers but ist administrators. They observe and write down what must happen according to elementary laws. As a group they form a transcription, as it were, of the horoscope under which all that comes into existence lives and dies, the last role assigned in ancient art to the old birth-goddesses. More than ever, it is their place to be present at the birth of a human being, not only on the Prometheus sarcophagi but also in cycles which represent the real curriculum vitae of a high state-official, or the upbringing of a child;[52] there the group of Parcae is easily recog-

---

[49] Robert, *op. cit.* 449, no. 357ᵃ. The sundial is similarly included in the death scene on a round altar, British Mus. no. 710, here Pl. XXVII. Museum photograph. She is isolated, but Hermes Psychopompos points to her to indicate that the hour of death has arrived.

[50] Account of the intellectual situation given in Gundel, *Entwicklungsgeschichte* 71 ff.

[51] Seneca, *Oedipus* 988: Primusque dies dedit extremum.

[52] Here are some examples, but the list does not claim to be complete:
(1) Florence, short side of sarcophagus with sacrifice of bull, *WV* 1888, pl. 9, no. 5 c, a poor drawing.
(2) Rome, San Lorenzo Fuori, *WV op. cit.* no. 4 b. Matz-Duhn 2, 332, 1. *Nbs.* There the round object is called a mirror.
(3) Rome, Villa Doria Pamfili. F. Cumont, *Syria* 10 (1929) pl. 43, 1. MD 2, 328, no. 3087. L. Deubner, *RömMitt* 27 (1912) 9 f.
(4) Paris, Louvre. Photo Giraudon no. 29457.

nized. Their outward appearance so closely resembles that of the Muses, who often stand next to them, that the real meaning of the scene becomes clear only through the iconographical context. On one end of the sarcophagus in Florence showing the sacrifice of a bull (Pl. XXVIII) the new-born baby is brought to the mother by a nurse wearing a head-cloth;[53] in the background two girlish figures are busy studying the globe; like the third, who is holding up a mask, one might take them to be Muses. Yet usually not two of the nine Muses are concerned with the celestial sphere, which is here placed on a pillar between the two at eye level, as the object of their inquiry. In fact, only two Moirai can be meant: again they read, as on the Vatican fragment, the horoscope of the new-born child, the one on the left holding a radius.[54] The same activity is clear on the otherwise quite crude sarcophagus in the Louvre (Pl. XXIX) where, in the background of the birth scene,[55] the sister with the scroll is again present assisting her. However, the venerable spinner is omitted, being superfluous in both cases. Neither does she appear on the sarcophagus in the Villa Doria Pamfili (Pl. XXX), even though all three Parcae are recognizably represented. On a pillar at the left, a sundial and sphere are set close together;[56] the first Moira manipulates a little stick. She communicates her observations to the other two, who stand directly behind her; the second one holds the previously mentioned tablet,[57] the third a scroll. Nemesis follows with wheel and measuring stick,[58] wearing a diadem signifying her position as matron and ruler. Once more the Moirai are assigned to her attendants, just as they serve Ananke in Plato. To our amazement we perceive the extraordinary constance of the concept which here still preserves the memory of the primal nature of the three goddesses as helpmeets. Yet we must not forget that exactly this human-mythical interrelation of the four person-

---

[53] Head scarf, as *RömMitt* 48 (1933) 177 ff.

[54] The photo, Pl. XXVIII, is from the archives of the Corpus of Sarcophagi. Courtesy G. Rodenwaldt.

[55] Raising up of the new-born infant corresponding to the usual explanation of "Levana"; cf. Dieterich, *Mutter Erde* 6.

[56] By the restorer? Cf. Matz-Duhn *loc. cit.*

[57] Left arm from wrist up seems to be modern.

[58] B. Schweitzer, *JdI* 46, (1931) 197.

ages made it possible symbolically to express the division of the once homogeneous concept of fate that had in the meantime taken place symbolically in thought. Will and fulfilment are its two aspects: the first could be left to the superior Ananke, the other to the planets.[59] Art thus gained for its long familiar images a new wealth of associations, gradually separating itself in the form of allegory from its mythical tasks and limitations. The heavens themselves undergo a strange metaphorical transformation and become the book of fate where the Moirai write down the irrevocable;[60] some of the stages of this process could be observed here. Thus ends the history of their representation in the almost complete abandonment of their original attributes, among which even the spindle is frequently missing. They are assembled around the image of the sphere as their real centre; originating in entirely different connections, the sphere was inseparably, though gradually, united with them. The allegorical seed planted so long ago put forth its own blossoms. The freedom of new artistic invention unfolds from the allegorical image, and between interpretation and appearance the network of countless inner relations comes into being. Thereby, the linkage of the individual to the cosmos could be represented: the simple figures of the girls with the sphere and sundial stood for the very idea of the common fate of mankind.

---

[59] Gundel, *op. cit.* 78. Equation of goddesses of fate Ananke and Nemesis, *ibid.* 73.

[60] *Ibid.*, 91.

INDEX

Acilius altar   59, 60, 63   see altar
Acrocorinth   39
Adrasteia   68
Aeschylus   38n.
Aetios   37n.
Aglaurids   81n.
Aion   37n., 40n.
Aisa   56
Alain de Lille   29
altar, Acilius   59, 60, 63
   Capitoline   57-58
Amasis   17-18
Ananke   36-38, 51, 54, 54n., 55-57, 61-62, 62n., 68, 74, 85
   Orphic   68n.
   in Pythagoras   37n.
Anaxagoras   35n.
Anima   83
Apollo, Delphic   16
   as cosmocrator   53n.
   sanctuary of at Didyma   41
Apuleius   41n.
Aquinas, Saint Thomas   29-29n.
Arachne   14n.
Archimedes, sphaira of   64n.
Ares   76-77
Aristophanes, Frogs 449   81
Aristotle   12n., 25, 33
   Metaph. 1, 5, 986b   18, 27n.
Artemis, Ephesian   58, 61
   Delphic cult of   61n.
Artemision, Ephesian, statuette from   60
Atargatis   60
Athena
   Elic   75n.
   of Erythrae   59
   of Ilium   59-60
Atropos   73, 82
   successor of   72
Augustine, Conf.   2, 4
Ausonius, Ludus septem Sapientium   17n.

Balzac   26   see E. R. Curtius
Bias   17, 42, 48n.
   head of   43
Bonaventura   29

calendar picture, see El Acabóse   66n.
Callimachus   41, 44
Cardinal Bembo   32
Cassirer, E.   28
Castiglione, B.   32
Chronos   33-35
   of Pythagoras   37
Cicero   32
Clotho   72, 73n., 82
coins
   from Hierapolis   60n.
   of Julia Domna   59
   with spindle of Taras   60n.
   of Uranopolis   53n.   see Urania
Colotes   74-75, 77
cosmic law, Empedocles'   37   see Empedocles
cosmocrator   15n., 53n.   see Apollo
cosmos   55
   periphery of   54
   spherical form of   27
Croesus   16n.
Curtius, E. R.   26
Cusanus   28n., 29
Cybele   58
Cynics   21, 43, 46

Dante   29
Dea Syria   57, 61, 63
Demetrius of Phaleron   7-8
Diogenes Laertius   19, 21, 30n., 41n.
   Vita of Thales   24n., 31
Dionysos   74-75, 77
Dolichenus, Aventine   58

El Acabóse, calendar picture from 66n.
Eleatics 25
Empedocles 37n.
Ephoros 16n.
Er 51, 61-62
Erinys 68
Eudoxus 14n.
Eukleides 24n.
Euripides 37n., 38n.

Ficino, Marsilio 29, 29n., 30n., 32n., 33n., 35
    letters of 36n.

George, Stefan 26
God 22, 26, 28, 28n., 36
    creation of 31
    form of 27
    is Aion, Kosmos, Chronos, Genesis 40n.
Goethe 12n., 37
    Faust 15
    Elective Affinities 32
Gundolf, F. 26

Hades 74, 78, 80
Hera 58
    from Ankyra 60n.
herm, Vatican 42, 44
    Ny-Carlsb. Glyptot. 43, 44
Hermes 15, 77
Herodotus 16
Hesiod 6
Hierapolis-Bambyke
    temple at 57
    statue at 59
    cult at 60
Hiero of Alexandria 64n.
Hippasus 31n.
Hippolytos 20, 27n.
Homer 6

Iamblichus 21, 37n.
Isis-Aion 25
Isocrates, tomb of 6

John the Baptist 42

Kassner, R. 26
Kepler, J. 28
Κλῶθες 57
Kosmos 34, 34n., 35, 40n.
Kratylos 34n.

Lachesis 72n., 73, 82
Linus 78
Lucian 57-61
Lydus, J. 80
Lysippus 45

Macrobius 28, 35n.
Madrid puteal 72-73
Manilius, M. 25
Mann, Th. 26n.
Marasch, Hittite reliefs from 61
Marcus Aurelius 32
    bronze coin of 60n.
Mariette drawing 42-43
Martial 73n.
Martianus Capella 82
Mechthild von Magdeburg 28-29
Meister Eckhart 29
Menander 8
Mithraic theology 38n.
Moira, Moirai, Ch. V
Mosaic
    Naples 1, 3-4, 8-9, 11n., 13-15, 42, 44
    Torre Annunziata 1, 8, 13, 43
    Villa Albani 1, 3-4, 7-8, 10n., 12, 15
    Monnus 14
    Isle of Wight 14
    Sainte Colombe 63n.

Necessity 36, 38, 50-51, 54-55, 74
    see Ananke
Nemesis 73n., 84
Nimrud, reliefs from 60
Nous 23, 35-36
Ny-Carlsberg Glyptothek, head in 43
Nymphs 56, 74-75, 79, 81 see Persephone

Ocellus Lucanus 25n.

Olympia, Heraion at   74
orb of the Holy Roman Empire   53
Origen   32
Orpheus   35, 79
Orphic elements   19, 68, 78, 80
Orphic hymns   26, 27n., 35n., 61

palm branch   43-45, 48
Pandrosos   78n.
Panthea   58   see Hera
Parcae, Ch. V
Paredros   58   see Dolichenus
Pascal   29
Pausanias   39n., 74n., 75
Periander   39, 42, 47   see portraits
   of
Persephone   68, 74-77, 79
   nymphs of   81
Pherecydes   27n., 34
Philolaus   36n.
Pindar   34n., 43-44
Pittakos   42
Plato   35, 50-51, 62-63
   Critias   31
   Politeia   38n.
   Protagoras   17n.
   Timaeus   25, 28n., 29n., 30-32,
      52, 54
Plotinus   34n.
Plutarch   19, 21, 23, 24n., 26, 27n.,
   30, 33, 35n.
   banquet of   17, 39
Pluto   74-75
Porphyrios   77n.
portraits of
   Euripides   49
   Periander   42, 47
   Pindar   43-44
   Pittakos   42
   Plato   49
   Socrates   49
   Sophocles   49
   Thales   48-49
Proclus   34n., 37n., 38
Prometheus sarcophagi   81, 83
Pythagoras   30n., 35, 37n.
   Chronos of   37
Pythagoreans   64n.

Pythagorean beliefs   64, 68

Rabelais   29
radius   11, 13, 15, 73, 82
Reisch, G.   26, 30
reliefs
   Colonna   71n.
   Dresnay Coll.   70, 73
   Locrian   75, 77, 79-80
   Marasch   61
   Mynno, tomb rel. of   63n.
   Nimrud   60
   votive rel., Aventine Dolichenus
      58

Sacrobosco   26, 29, 31
Sarapis   28
Selene   58
Serapeum in Memphis   41, 43n.
Seuse   29
Seven Sages, Ch. I-II
   portraits of   45-49
Simonides   38n.
Stagel, E.   28
St. Benedict   28
Stobaeus   19-20, 36
Stoics   35, 37n.

Thales   24, 27, 33, 36, 38, 39   and
   Ch. III
   aphorisms by   22, 26, 30, 33

Urania   11, 14-15, 61, 73, 82
   on coins   53n.
   from House of the Vettii   13,
      15

Vergil   11

Winckelmann   1
world soul   35, 36n., 37, 54

Xenophanes   27, 35n.

Zeus   34, 58
   infant   79
   as bull   80

LIST OF PLATES

I   Philosopher mosaic from Torre Annunziata. Naples, National Museum. Photograph: Alinari 12199.

II-VI.   Details of the same mosaic.

VII.   Philosopher mosaic. Rome, Villa Albani. Photograph: Prof. Dr. Hellmut Sichtermann; DAI, Rome, Neg. Nr. 2143a.

VIII.   Sarcophagus. Munich, Glyptothek, Inv. no 326. Photograph: after Kaufmann, *Amtliche Ausgabe* 169.

IX.   Urania. Painting from Pompeii, Casa dei Vettii. Photograph: after *MonAnt* 8, 1898, 278, pl. 17.

X.   Roman mosaic, detail. From the Isle of Wight. Photograph: after Morgan, *Romano-British Mosaik Pavements*, pl. 21.

XI.   Funerary relief. Istanbul, Archaeological Museum. Photograph: by kind permission of the Museum authorities.

XII.   "La bellezza." Design of Cesare Ripa.

XIII-XIV.   Marble herm in the Ny-Carlsberg Glyptotek, inv. no 424. Photographs: kindly provided by Prof. Dr. F. Poulsen.

XV-XVI.   Marble herm. Rome, Museo Nazionale delle Terme. Photographs: DAI, Rome, Neg. Nr. 8082.

XVII.   Apollo. Painting from Pompeii, Casa dell'Argenteria.

XVIII.   Marble altar. Rome, Capitoline Museum. Photograph: kindly provided by Prof. Dr. Carlo Pietrangeli.

XIX.   Terracotta medallion. Brindisi, Archaeological Museum. Photograph: after M. J. Vermaseren, *Liber in deum* (EPRO 53), Leiden 1976, pl. XXXIII.

XX.   Relief from Marash. Istanbul, Archaeological Museum. Photograph: after Humann-Puchstein, *Reisen in Kleinasien*, pl. 45.

XXI.   Bone whorl. London, British Museum, inv. no G 413. Photographs: by kind permission of the Museum authorities.

XXII. Bronze whorl. Naples, National Museum. Photograph: by kind permission of the Museum authorities.

XXIII. Marble relief with the representation of the Parcae. Dresnay Collection, Château du Dréneuc (Loire inférieure). Photograph: DAI, Rome.

XXIV. Terracotta relief from Locri. Reggio Calabria, Archaeological Museum. Photograph: after *Archivio Storico per la Calabria e la Lucania, In Memoriam P. Orsi*, pl. 14.

XXV. Detail of a rhyton from Southern Italy. London, British Museum, inv. no F 426. Photograph: kindly provided by the Museum authorities.

XXVI. Fragment of a sarcophagus in the Vatican Musea. Photograph: after C. Robert, *Die antiken Sarkophagreliefs*, no 354.

XXVII. Round altar. London, British Museum, inv. no 710. Photograph: kindly provided by the Museum authorities.

XXVIII. Sarcophagus, shortside. Florence, Uffizi. Photograph: DAI, Rome, Neg. Nr. 57.611.

XXIX. Sarcophagus. Paris, Louvre, inv. no MA 319. Photograph: kindly provided by the Museum authorities (Giraudon 29457).

XXX. Sarcophagus. Rome, Villa Doria Pamfili. Photograph: DAI, Rome, Neg. Nr. 8332.

PLATE I

PLATE II

PLATE III

PLATE IV

I

2

PLATE V

PLATE VI

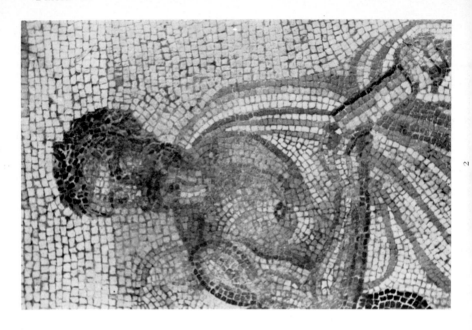

PLATE VII

PLATE VIII

PLATE IX

PLATE X

PLATE XI

PLATE XII

PLATE XIII

PLATE XIV

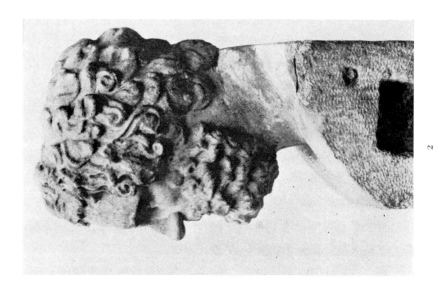

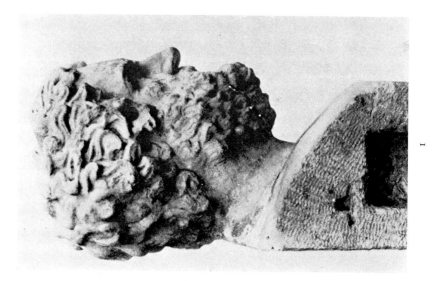

PLATE XV

PLATE XVI

2

1

PLATE XVII

PLATE XVIII

PLATE XIX

PLATE XX

PLATE XXI

1

2

PLATE XXII

PLATE XXIII

PLATE XXIV

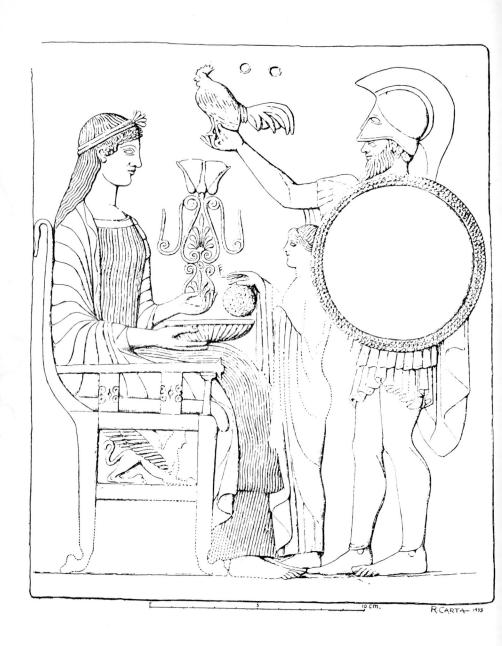

PLATE XXV

PLATE XXVI

PLATE XXVII

PLATE XXVIII

PLATE XXIX

PLATE XXX